PATIENCE & GRATITUDE

STORIES OF HEALING

YOHANNA ABDULLAH

PARTRIDGE

Print information available on the last page.

To order additional copies of this book, contact
Toll Free +65 3165 7531 (Singapore)
Toll Free +60 3 3099 4412 (Malaysia)
orders.singapore@partridgepublishing.com

www.partridgepublishing.com/singapore

CONTENTS

To Mak who has borne me with patient constancy

ACKNOWLEDGEMENTS

The Author would like to express her deepest appreciation to the following:

1. Her Excellency Halimah Yacob, President of the Republic of Singapore, for kindly writing the Foreword.

2. Prof Chua Hong Choon, Dr Radiah Salim, Ustazah Shameen Sultanah binte Abdul Ghafoor, Shari Almashoor, Nurleen Mohamad, Yogeswaran Muniyanda, Mohamad Rosli Bin Abu Bakar (Anjang), Lee Shermin, Haslinah Osman, Kate Loreto, Nur Marina Abdullah Chong, Roszita Bte Idrus, Sarinah Said, Nur Afiqah bte Mohd Azman, Ella Mohd, Derrick Looi Leong Kit, Sumaiyah Mohamed, Faizal Abdul Rahim, Siti Hazirah Binte Mohamad for sharing their stories.

3. Ms Noorunnisa d/o PK Ibrahim Kutty for editing the contents of this book.

FOREWORD

Club HEAL has played an active role in raising awareness and educating the community about people with mental health challenges. Through their publications, Club HEAL aims to empathise with, encourage and empower people with mental health challenges. I am glad to be able to contribute to Club HEAL's sixth book, *Patience and Gratitude*.

This book examines the values of patience and gratitude in the healing and recovery of people with mental health challenges, seen through the stories of people in recovery as they courageously overcome the battles and difficulties in their lives. Sometimes, the challenges in our lives do not come with simple solutions. The mountain ahead may seem insurmountable, and the wisdom from life's challenges may come much later on. Practising patience and gratitude can help us to feel at peace with the past, joy in the present, and hope for the future.

The stories of the various individuals in this book and their journeys of healing and recovery are all unique. Anyone and everyone can come away from this book with lessons learned. I hope that the generous sharing in this book brings you further ahead in your journey of self-discovery and healing.

Thank you to the contributors of the stories in this book for the uplifting read. You have reminded us of what it means to live our lives with patience and gratitude. Regardless of our challenges, as long as we persevere, remain grounded and be thankful, we will get through it all. Let us draw inspiration from these stories, and be grateful that we can all contribute to the world, with all we have learnt and gained.

HALIMAH YACOB
PRESIDENT OF THE REPUBLIC OF SINGAPORE

REBIRTH

I am reborn
By your Fire
Transformed
I change lives
In exchange for lies
That blind true faith
I know
I can fly
Above my sorrows
Scale mountains high
Dive into oceans deep
For with you I have the strength
To see my trials as roads to heaven
I am not alone
With you I am healed
With you I AM
Triumphant

Yohanna Abdullah
15.7.2020

PREFACE

YOHANNA ABDULLAH

I am a patient patient. I believe so, having coped with bipolar disorder for 22 years. When my psychiatrist said in 2019, "Yohanna, let's get you well for another 20 years", I was aghast. That is a lifetime of struggle to stay well and not have severe symptoms that will land me in hospital.

Having experienced the most extremes of highs and lows and witnessing all its disadvantages – not being able to get out of bed even for a bath or a meal, to crazily spending money on unnecessary things like buying a car when I don't know how to drive, or taking a debt to buy an OSIM massage chair and other unnecessary items salespersons convince me to purchase in my irrational mood – I am grateful that I am sane for most of the time. That I can spend time with my family, friends, and colleagues as a 'normal' human being. Having walked through fire and having lived experience of mental illness, I am grateful to be a mental health advocate with Club HEAL from its inception in 2012. It has been an incredible and most gratifying journey and I am ready to contribute even more in the years to come.

I am grateful for the opportunity to pen four books with Club HEAL – *Shattered, We Heal* (2014), *Shattered, We Heal II* (2015), *Mind at Peace* (2016) and *A Place in the Sun* (2018), which are all also available in Malay. The first book, which was also translated into Mandarin, was quickly sold out. *Alhamdulillah* (Praises be to God), our books have helped many to understand the plight of the mentally ill and their caregivers through touching and inspiring stories of life's ups and downs.

That is why I am excited about my fifth book with Club HEAL, *Patience and Gratitude – Stories of Healing;* it contains profiles of people whose health and other challenges affected their mental well-being.

As my mentor and sister-in-Islam, President of Club HEAL, Dr. Radiah Salim, pointed out to me, there is a difference between healing and recovery. Recovery is the absence of symptoms for a length of time, be it a year, a few years or till the end of one's life. Having recovered, one can still suffer a relapse, after which the striving to recovery begins again. Healing is a process of recovery from the traumas of life, the emotional, spiritual, mental and lastly physical pain that one undergoes, sometimes from childhood, through maybe abuse, abandonment, the loss of loved ones, bullying and illnesses of the mind, body and soul. Wounded, we *can* heal, even as the scars remain.

In this book, we bring you the most intimate stories of people who have walked the mile yet remain whole – who are mending the cracks in their lives and emerging from their brokenness, trials and tribulations triumphant – because of their embodiment of the spirit of patience and gratitude. Patience takes time and the determination to accept whatever comes our way, and bear them without much complaint, surrendering to the Wisdom of a Higher Power.

Being grateful means being thankful for the small and little things in life: every breath that enables us to live a moment longer; our senses which allow us to enjoy the company of loved ones and nature and even man-made pleasures; and our physical bodies that enable us to partake of these pleasures. A smart phone that brings the world to us when we are stuck at home, the bus driver who greets and smiles as we venture out, a glass of cold water when we are thirsty – the list of things we have that fulfils our needs and wants is long, and that is in itself a reason to be happy.

Do read these 15 stories of people who are both patient and grateful, who have learned to foster happiness and peace of mind in going through their daily challenges. Four others have been in the position to help others heal. We challenge you to learn from them and be patient and grateful too in your journeys of healing and recovery.

May peace be upon you.

INTRODUCTION

DR RADIAH SALIM

"No one has been given a better and more ample gift than endurance." [Bukhari]

Both patience and gratitude play very important roles in the healing and recovery processes of a person facing a health challenge and in increasing his endurance.

Patience

Patience is a virtue. A patient person will not give up in the face of life's challenges, including health challenges.

"Be sure We shall test you with something of fear and hunger, or some loss in goods or lives or the fruits (of your toil); but

> give glad tidings to those who patiently
> persevere – (those) who say, when afflicted
> with calamity: **'To God we belong, and
> to Him is our return'**. They are those on
> whom blessings from God (descend), and
> Mercy, and they are the ones who receive
> guidance." [al-Baqarah: 155-157]

A patient person does not complain much because he believes Allah will not burden him more than he can bear.

> "On no soul does God place a burden
> greater than it can bear …" [al-
> Baqarah: 286]

The patient person is confident of Allah's help.

> "O you who have believed, seek help
> through patience and prayer. Indeed, Allah
> is with the patient." [al-Baqarah: 153]

Solat (Prayer) and Discipline

Solat teaches a person to be disciplined. The person who prays will be more diligent in looking for treatment and adhering to it.

In managing an illness, practicing a healthy lifestyle is very important – such as taking nutritious food, exercise, rest and sleep, tackling life's stressors and avoiding harmful habits such as smoking or alcohol consumption. This requires discipline and an ability to control our desires – qualities of a patient person.

Also, the patient person will be disciplined in keeping appointments with a health professional such as a doctor, a nurse, a social worker or a counsellor. Taking medicine consistently also requires patience.

The patient person, whether he is the one facing the health challenge or the caregiver, will also reduce stress to himself and others. He will not be in a hurry or put pressure on himself or others in going through the recovery process, because he realizes that the recovery process requires time and discipline.

> *"Verily, with every difficulty there is relief"*
> [al-Insyirah: 6]

Gratitude

Gratitude is also a virtue. The person who has gratitude is thankful for any treatment available. He is determined to benefit from therapy as much as possible. This person is sure of Allah's help, because, as Allah has promised, every illness has a remedy.

> *"Allah has not sent down a disease without sending a cure for it."* – [Bukhari]

A grateful person seeks the wisdom behind every challenge he faces. For example, he realizes that challenges can wipe away sins, or be a means to develop humility. This in turn elevates his status in the eyes of Allah and brings the person closer to Him.

This person is also more likely to understand better others facing the same challenge. It gives him the strength to help others when he recovers. He has more empathy because he too has walked the path. He is therefore a more effective caregiver due to his own experience with the illness.

This is why, we in Club HEAL do not just have an 'equal opportunities' policy when it comes to hiring staff or volunteers from among those who have experienced illness as patients or as caregivers, we favour them. They are a source of inspiration. They embody hope.

1

THE PRICE OF FREEDOM IS PRICELESS

Freedom is priceless for Yogeswaran Muniyanda, 47, a peer at Club HEAL, for he spent his youth and prime years behind bars. The reason? Abusing drugs since he was 16, after mixing with bad company and joining a gang. His first taste of life behind bars was in a detention barrack during National Service when he was jailed after going AWOL (absence without official leave) and consuming drugs. This started a series of imprisonment at DRCs (Drug Rehabilitation Centres) and prisons.

Yoges (as he is called at Club HEAL where he has been as a peer since October 2017), suspects he was suffering from depression even as a child, but he was officially diagnosed with schizophrenia only in prison.

"My father was also a schizophrenic, an alcoholic and a drug addict. And he was an abusive parent. My mom and dad were always quarrelling," explained Yoges, pointing to these family issues as the root of his psychiatric illness.

Gangsterism in and out of jail

His drug addiction and involvement with gangs as a teenager was the outlet for his confusion, depression, and anger at that time. "I had no one to talk to, not my mother, brother, nor my friends. I was not mature enough to seek help." He finally stopped the habit at the age of 33 while in prison. Before that, in between the sentences to imprisonment, he still reverted to his bad habits of relying on drugs and his gang members, who frequently got into fights with other gangs.

Ironically, life in prison was also not without gangsterism – and blatant racism. "The Malays were locked in one cell, the Chinese, in their own cell and the Indians in another. If they were in mixed cells, they would fight with one another."

In DRCs though, there were about 100 people in one big dormitory. Fights were frequent, but they would be stopped by armed wardens. Though there were many people to befriend, Yoges was unable to share his feelings with anyone. "I did not want fellow inmates to know about my illness and life. The only relief I had was during recreation times in the hall and in the yard, where I would play basketball."

Mental pain worse than physical pain

One of the most horrific moments was when he was caned a total of 39 strokes over a period of more than 10 years, while serving Long Term Imprisonment 1 and 2 (LT1 and LT2). "It was very painful. I controlled the pain by breathing. But mental pain is even worse."

His depression developed into schizophrenia when he started hearing voices while in the Isolation Cell. "A voice kept calling me and it would not stop talking. It repeated over and over again that I was condemned to death sentence. I started meditating and became convinced I was a Yogi and a Buddha who had had attained enlightenment. I named myself Yin and Yang. The psychiatrist was called. He gave me injections and medicines to stop the voice and I was put in the psychiatric ward."

"There, it was much better, as there were only around 10 people in the ward. Nevertheless, we were handcuffed to our beds because we were aggressive and would still have fought with each other given a chance."

Mom's loving patience

His mother was his most frequent and devoted visitor all his 20 years behind bars. She faithfully saw him every two weeks. Rajeswathy d/o Chellum Perumal, 64, said that she routinely did this for the love of her son and was very distraught when she was not allowed to do so at times because he was too ill to see her. "His condition grew worse and I would sit and cry and write letters to the authorities to be given permission to see him. But sometimes, he himself refused to see me."

Yoges suffered a further blow when he developed a huge tumour on his left knee and had to replace part of his leg with metal. Said Rajeswathy, "I was shocked to see him on a wheelchair one day. Soon after, he was warded for two weeks at the Singapore General Hospital. During that time, he didn't know himself, did not know where he was, and did not bathe. They had to take out part of his leg and replace it with metal. He had to do the operation as he would otherwise suffer from terrible back pain. Now, his left leg is shorter than the other and he walks with difficulty using a walking stick."

After his last day in prison, he was immediately sent to IMH (Institute of Mental Health), where he remained for one year, to be treated for schizophrenia. "I may have been freed from prison, but my mind was still not free," he lamented. He has been living with his mother since discharge from that institution.

Rajeswathy admits it has not been easy for her. "If you think he had it tough, as a caregiver it is three times harder, no, 300 times more difficult. When he was in prison, I would visit him every two weeks, never missing. I would advise him not to do bad things. It was very painful to see my son behind bars."

She remembers him as a playful child who performed very well in school until Primary Six when he started mixing with bad company and became difficult for her to control. He dropped out of school in Secondary Two but resumed his studies and graduated from ITE (Institute of Technological Education).

When Yoges came out of prison, caring for him while she was working was physically and mentally draining. "His leg was infected and there was pus and he could have had his leg amputated but I helped treat the infection. I was under a lot of stress. He kept on talking and talking. He believed he could fly. I couldn't sleep because he would wake me up in the night to go to the temple. At times I feared for him and for myself. At times, I needed to work the next day and would badly need my sleep. Then I would call the ambulance to take him to IMH."

Better days at Club HEAL

After becoming a peer at Club HEAL for three years, things have started looking up for Yoges and his mom. "I feel relieved that so many problems that I had with him are gone. He can go himself to places by himself, his pain is reduced, he doesn't isolate himself. I see a lot of changes since he joined Club HEAL," said Rajeswathy.

Yoges himself testifies to his transformation at Club HEAL. "I have not had a relapse since I came to Club HEAL. Even when I suffer from mental and physical pain now and then, I can control myself. I feel that I am getting better day by day. In the morning I wake up, get ready and go to Club HEAL. Today, I had Aneez Fathima's yoga session and I was with the programme executives, Supinah and Derrick and all the other peers. I have my own way of meditation, so I did not follow Aneez's teachings. She is a very nice lady and very friendly too and knows much about yoga which she learnt from an Indian guru. She teaches the peers step by step."

Yoges does his own meditation during Aneez's session. "For 13 years, while I was in prison, I learned from myself to do meditation. I simply sit and keep silent for hours."

Another of the rehabilitation session that he enjoys is Shari's. "She taught us self-awareness and reinforced my belief in the Law of Karma. She is my guru as are Aneez, Zainal and Yohanna – my other beloved gurus who teach us different things. They have taught me to accept my past, move on and forgive those who hurt me, especially my father."

Forgiveness brings peace

Forgiving his father, whom he blamed for his unhappy past, unconditionally became possible when fellow peers and staff convinced him to let go of his anger. "I feel positive energy at Club HEAL because every one of us has gone through similar experiences, and I know they are here to support me. Every day at Club HEAL I get the energy to revitalise myself," he enthused.

Yoges feels he has managed to grow emotionally at Club HEAL. Initially seen as a 'philosopher' espousing multiple incoherent ideas, Yoges has now become more focused and is able to convey his ideas in a way that others can understand. His worldview is encapsulated in phrase, "Pain, Pleasure, Peace and Love." He writes poems to share his messages and has taken further steps to pursue his interests, including learning guitar at Faith Music School, which teaches those with mental and physical disabilities at no cost. As he is paid for attending these classes by SG Enable, a government set-up that looks after the physically disabled in Singapore, he faithfully attends each class despite the distance from his home, and notwithstanding the physical pain he suffers daily.

SG Enable is also financing half of his $5,000 course fee for a certificate in Digital Marketing, which he has enrolled in with the help of Club HEAL. The other half of the fee is paid by his Skills Future Singapore. "I find the course very interesting and enlightening and I was told that upon completion, I will be assisted in getting a suitable job."

Dream job

While things are looking up for Yoges, he still looks forward to ultimately attaining his dream job – to be an addictions counsellor at Club HEAL. "I wish to help rehabilitate drug addicts, help them give up their addiction. Many are suffering from mental health conditions. I want to give them hope to lead a new life. Drug addicts are treated like criminals, my experience testifies to that. I want the laws to be changed so that drug addicts are no longer treated as convicts but as people who need help to rebuild their lives.

Yoges believes that one day he can achieve his ambition with the support of Club HEAL. For Yoges, the H in HEAL stands for the hope he has in his healing and recovery from schizophrenia. E means being equipped with the tools to foster and sustain mental and physical health. A means accepting his past, learning from it and preparing for a better future. "L stands for the LOVE that I receive from my friends in Club HEAL, who have become the family I never had," said Yoges.

Inculcating patience and gratitude

"I was very impatient when I was young but my journey especially with imprisonment and struggles with mental health issues have made me a very patient person."

Rajeswathy agrees, noting that his challenges have been overwhelming. "If not for his patience and gratitude, he could not have survived."

Yoges recognises the pivotal role his mother plays in his healing and recovery. "Every day, I tell my mother, 'I love you. Thank you for taking care of me.'" Her unconditional love and patience and sacrifices motivates him to be patient as well, taking one day at a time.

"'Patience and Gratitude' is our mantra," assert both mother and son.

A dream family life

Like every normal person, Yoges also has dreams of having a family life. "Once I have a steady job, I want to have a family and children. I have been in love before and I know what it is like. I am a normal person too and I have feelings. Moreover, I want my mum to have someone to take care of her when she becomes older. I am asking her to please get a bride for me."

Rajeswathy, however, refuses to entertain this wish for the time being. "I tell him to take one thing at a time. Get a job, save enough money, then only we can talk. Women nowadays are not like those of my time who will stick with marriage through thick and thin. Money matters."

Yoges knows his mother is right and plans to just do his best. He will patiently wait for his wounds to heal even as they leave scars. "I no longer get upset when I think of the past. But I do regret taking drugs and I want to help youths stop their addiction. I went to SINDA asking if they need any volunteers, but they didn't have an opening at the time. They helped me apply for further financial assistance instead."

Yoges and his mother are nevertheless happy with his current state of progress as he trudges painfully forward with his cane along the arduous road of his healing and recovery. And as he slowly sees his dreams being fulfilled one by one, he is indeed, most grateful.

2

CONQUERING THE DEMONS OF DEMENTIA

My name is Mohamad Rosli Bin Abu Bakar and I am 56 years old. I am known as Anjang and I am an advocate for a dementia-friendly society. For eight years I had been suffering from severe headaches and other symptoms but was diagnosed with Young Onset Dementia only in 2017. It was frightening to be diagnosed with the condition, which affects people below the age of 65.

Then, I was at my prime, in my forties and holding a lucrative job as a superintendent in an international chemical plant in Jurong Island but I decided to quit as I progressively became confused and could not multi-task anymore. The prospect of being unproductive at a young age – of knowing I was going to be incrementally robbed of my cognitive abilities and emotional awareness was horrifying.

I have lost many friendships over the years, plus my pride, self-esteem and much more. It was a nightmare – the hallucination, delusion, depression, humiliation, – yet I had to carry on with my financial responsibilities to my family and live life to my fullest potential.

I am jobless, and worry about the next meal for my family, about medical expenses and keeping up with doctors' appointments.

I used to be eloquent but now it is difficult to express myself and have a decent conversation. It is frustrating and slowly kills my desire to communicate. Writing, which was once a pleasure, is now a lost art and very laborious.

Even so, I am trying to sustain my sanity, trying my best to remember events in my life, which have shaped me. I refuse to wave the white flag; I am a hardened warrior and am still on the battlefield fighting my "enemy". But I do know this is a terminal illness – it will progressively walk me to my last resting place.

The best caregiver

To live under the same roof with a dementia-disabled person is challenging and frustrating due to the strong emotional attachment between caregiver and patient. If the caregiver is not well-equipped with relevant skills, it can be chaotic, with many conflicts and arguments. Emotional distress can lead to mental and physical exhaustion. It can cause both parties to be drowned in a pessimistic outlook on life, with disastrous results. People with dementia need loving care, and need to be given confidence, dignity, and respect.

So long as I can, I wish to help my primary caregiver, my wife, help me. So, my wife and I attend dementia workshops, mini-forums and sharing sessions together, where we listen to other caregivers' experiences and pick the best practices of caregiving. She has become the best caregiver I could ask for, and a major support in my life.

Beating the odds

Although I know there is no known cure for dementia, there is no point waiting for my "death sentence". Have a sweet denial period, grieve as much as you want – you deserve so much if you are diagnosed with a terminal illness. But take charge of your life again after that. It is not the end of the world.

Many are surprised to see that I am trying to live life as normal as possible. Many people comment, "You do not look like you are having dementia". "You look normal to me". These comments used to hurt me but not anymore. It gives me a sense of achievement as it takes tremendous efforts to stay focused and strong. So, I am not going to admit defeat – that is a very vital and important attitude for both the person with dementia and the caregiver.

I study the triggers to my hallucination, delusion, depression, anxiety, apathy, suicide ideation and many more. Since I have Parkinson's as well, I also monitor my motor problems. I take notes and chart all vital information about my illnesses. Patience is of the utmost importance because while doing the monitoring, I need to withstand the full blow of the attacks at the same time.

Visualising success

While dementia affects my brain function, I still have the power to learn anew and reduce the impairment. I learn about the power of visualisation in healing and recovery to improve and re-program my brain function – whatever is left of it. I set schedules for visualisation exercises to reduce the number of triggers and attacks. It is a painful and tough process, but it is a journey worth taking. It is always mind over body.

Let the spirit soar

Conquering the mind over the body involves a spiritual journey of the heart and soul. I was a student of Sufism before I had dementia. The essence of the teaching is to cleanse and ensure your heart is not attached to worldly worries. I used these teachings to map for myself the route for my spiritual journey – powerful mind visualisation during the day and spiritual solace and enlightenment in the early hours of the night. The main objective is to release all worldly stress and ensure closeness to the Almighty. With this, I am better able to control and minimise the symptoms of my illnesses.

Seeing angels in the sky

In the past, I had horrific hallucinations and delusions. With the spiritual practices, I now have pleasurable hallucinations such as of angels visiting me, swirling from the far sky down and standing smiling in front of me. As my doctor says if I am enjoying my hallucinations, let it be. There are no more thousands of creepy crawlies on the floor, nor ugly faces standing before me.

However, I can still get suicidal thoughts and if I do, I will admit myself to Tan Tock Seng Hospital's psychiatric ward. I will get professional advice and assistance. I know well how these thoughts can harm me.

Nature's way

I also do research on alternative traditional remedies for my emotional and physical well-being. Modern medicines have side-effects on the mind and the body. Moreover, appointments with the neurologist last only about half an hour each time and are at four-month intervals, which is frankly insufficient. I have tried a few traditional herbs remedies with good results. I take turmeric powder, virgin coconut oil, black seed oil and Omega 3 as my alternative remedies. They lower my anxiety, depression, and improve my focus and sustain my cognitive function. Even though dementia will eventually take its toll on me completely, I am grateful I can still function as a normal person to a large extent up to now.

Maintaining independence

Since I am jobless and have plenty of free time, I produce turmeric powder supplements for friends and relatives for a modest income. I do not charge a fixed rate but receive sincere contributions. I produce a minimum of 1,500 capsules per month, the number of which is still increasing. With this activity, I am kept busy and productive rather than playing Bingo at a day care centre. My independence and wellbeing have far exceeded the expectations of my neurologist and other doctors at Tan Tock Seng Hospital, who had once asked my wife to prepare me to be admitted to a nursing home.

Active advocate

I keep on being productive with dementia advocacy work with Alzheimer's Disease Association Singapore (ADA). I am an advisor to Kebun Bahru Constituency's dementia-friendly project. I am creating awareness about dementia in the Malay community through The Chapal Malay Dementia Community, which I initiated, which recruits community volunteer leaders to do outreach. I have also joined Dementia Alliance International, Dementia Friends of New Zealand and am actively involved with the Kiama Municipal Town Council Dementia Friendly Advisory Board, Australia.

Sustainability

Sustaining one's mind and body and soul is the key to conquering the demons of dementia. It is a process which involves PATIENCE and GRATITUDE; patience in accepting my condition and gratitude to those caregivers who supported me. I need to continuously learn, practice my knowledge, and never say die.

The journey of HEALING and RECOVERY is tough. There are moments when I can be suicidal, but I try to resist with a strong faith and a powerful mind. I hold on to the hope that even if dementia kills me some day, I will be able to take this journey to the end as a person with DIGNITY and RESPECT. After all, everyone must die in one way or another. God willing, at the end of my journey, there are rays of sunshine that lead to paradise.

To my soulmate and beloved caregiver, Sarimah:

A journey is just the beginning of many happy experiences

It is the walk hand in hand that puts ease to the ailing heart

Contentment comes from the sincere support of loving caregivers

Who cry then laugh, who fall and rise again with grace and love

---

3

SINGING IN THE RAIN

She is a writer, she is a singer, she is Shermin. She is not bipolar. *Bipolar is her*, as she wrote in her book, which captures her experience as a person with bipolar disorder. Lee Shermin, 26, a part-time Programme Executive at Club HEAL, was diagnosed with the mental illness in 2017.

The delivery of her firstborn contributed to her illness. "I had a traumatic birth experience and couldn't sleep properly without sleeping pills." Her insomnia landed Shermin in the Institute of Mental Health for the first time three years ago, and since then, she has been hospitalised six times.

A loving husband and beautiful children

Maybe because the illness is still relatively new, Shermin is not exactly sure what her triggers are. This beautiful and big-hearted lady is grateful that she has the love and support of her husband, Desmond Jose, assistant general manager at an F&B outfit. They met when they were both working at Holland Village. "He was an operations manager and I was a singer at the opposite bar. We got married on 18 June 2015 and have been together since."

Desmond has been a pillar of support through all the times when she showed her worst symptoms of bipolar disorder. She is Type 1 Bipolar, which means she is more prone to mania, although, like all people with bipolar disorder, she may also sink to the depths of depression.

Said Shermin, "When I'm manic or depressive, I tell him, and he tries to make me feel better. Like the one time I woke up and couldn't sleep because I kept hearing songs non-stop in my head, like a radio with no ads. He made me hot Milo and we sat together, riding the mania storm."

The couple are blessed with two children, Eliza, who is turning 4, and Reyhan, who has just turned 2. "I don't like dealing with their fighting or crying, but every time my daughter hugs me and tells me she loves me, my spirits are lifted, and I feel I have meaning and purpose in this life (to love and be loved by my children)."

But as much as she loves her children and would like to have more, she is stopping at two. "If I didn't have to take medication, I would like to have another child as I want to re-live the breastfeeding experience."

Mood swings and healing

Shermin is by nature an expressive and loving woman. As she said, "I'm naturally loud and vibrant, but my mood is always swinging. I feel less animated now that I'm on medication, but more stable in terms of my mood swings (it swings less violently, and I've noticed my moods are more consistent, going from day to day)."

Considering her relapses, Shermin confesses she does not know which stage of healing she is at. "I'm just living each day as it comes. Healing is an active activity – it takes planning and effort. Once I have healed, then we can talk about recovery," she observes pragmatically.

For the time being, every day Shermin reminds herself to be patient with herself. "Drought or not, I can't control the rain. This is an analogy for how I can't control my luck and the opportunities that come my way – I can only stay patient and believe the good things will come. Thus, this poem."

Patience
By Shermin Lee

Patience, patience
I can't begin
To tell you how much
I want to win

Win at life
And be successful
How I yearn
To be my most useful

Yet here I am
Living day to day
Can't speed up time
Perhaps the only way

To make the wait bearable
From here to there
Is to live without knowing
When or where

In the here and now
I should try to remain
Drought or not
I can't control the rain

Shermin reflects on her emotions and shares her healing and recovery journey with others through her Instagram account @sherminukulee. It is a play on her name and the fact that she loves to play the ukulele and does so to brighten her days and of those around her. When she comes to Club HEAL, where she is a peer, she sashays with her infectious energy and sings and plays the ukulele for her friends at rehab.

Although Club HEAL mostly caters to the Muslim community, Shermin, who is "largely an agnostic", feels embraced by the counsellors, the staff, and the peers there. Here are her own words on her experience there.

Club HEAL: A Place Where Differences are Respected

By Shermin Lee

What did my first counsellor do when I told her I was low key, thinking suicidal thoughts, and needed to leave the premises?

She took me for a walk outside, and we ended up leaning back against a wall, clenching and opening our fists, breathing.

I spent hours talking with my second counsellor about Islam, and I raised extremely provocative questions about the faith she was born into and grew up nurturing.

Did she shut me down? No, she sat with me, and only closed the conversational thread once, when she had grown weary of taking my pointed questions.

And when I asked the club members if I could be included in their prayer session (the act of Salat), did they refuse me?

No. The three women (a counsellor and two peers) led and guided me through the process of practicing the Muslim prayer.

*This is what it means to be inclusive. Club HEAL is a great example of racial and religious **harmony**.*

Writing and singing lifts her spirit. "I keep a blog, and I post my singing with my ukulele on Instagram. I have a book on my manic episodes that landed me in hospital. You can purchase it at sherminleebook. blogspot.com. It is being illustrated by my sister."

Her family values her and helps her keep a positive outlook on life. "They support me. When I did not have a job, sometimes that makes me feel useless, but when I'm in their company, especially with my children, I feel useful again."

Showing up for a cause

Because of the still prevailing stigma against the mentally ill, Shermin notes that employment opportunities are limited. "I think employers are afraid to employ a person with a mental health condition, which is sad, because we can be productive, too, given the right environment."

So Shermin has put her talent and persona to good use as a mental health advocate, appearing in campaigns to fight the stigma against people with mental health issues. What does she do to help in this cause? Shermin answered with a shrug, "I just show up. That's the most important thing, to be relied on to show up and be present, and to not disappoint."

4

A BLESSED LIFE WITH HAPPY ENDINGS

This is no fairy tale, but it does have a happy ending for one determined lady who has struggled with mental illness since young. Haslinah Osman, 48, an author of Islamic children's books, has lost several loved ones and lived alone almost all her life, which contributed to her schizophrenia. She overcame her self-image of being fat and undesirable when she finally met her "knight in shining armour".

For nine years now, Haslinah has been happily married to a man who was matchmade by a friend. She was not in love with him before the marriage – which is now a long distance one – but has grown to love the man who showed much care and concern and helped her build her confidence and heal her deepest wounds.

Haslinah believes that her depression began when her mother died when she was at the tender age of ten. She said, "I had to come home after school and remain there all alone until late afternoon when my siblings returned. None of them detected my depression as I never cried in their presence. In fact, I used to look happy when surrounded by my little nieces and nephews."

Her condition worsened after her father died when she was 19. She had grown to love his companionship during his retirement, and his death was traumatic.

Poor self-image

In her teens and much through adulthood, Haslinah had a poor image of herself. "During my teenage years, I learnt that since I was fat and not pretty no one would fancy me, unlike my other classmates. Some of the boys would, in fact, use me as a messenger to send love letters and presents to my girl friends who were pretty and sweet."

She resolved then to work hard and build her career instead of wasting her life yearning for romance. Additionally, she planned to become a single mother to adoptive children. "I loved children but hated boys and men because they were biased against me and made fun of me."

Unfortunately, a spanner was thrown into the works when she was first diagnosed with schizophrenia at 27.

First heartbreak, first mental breakdown

At the age of 26, Haslinah left Singapore to start a new life in Brunei as a kindergarten teacher in an Islamic school. Her contract was for two years, but it ended after six months when her symptoms of schizophrenia surfaced after she fell in love. "I didn't expect my heart to feel for someone there. I was fighting off my feelings because I knew it was not going to work out since I knew I was not pretty enough to be fancied. I kept to myself and did not to mix around with the other teachers and staff. I was longing for love but did not believe it could be reciprocated. The owners of the kindergarten noticed my strange behaviour and sent me home. Of course, I felt more upset as a result; I felt their action was unjustified."

In Singapore, she lived in a rental flat in Hougang alone and studied at the National Institute of Education (NIE) to teach the Malay language. But things still did not move as planned. "I met a male teacher at NIE who was like the man that I fell in love with in Brunei. I was convinced that all the other students knew my thoughts and were mocking me behind my back. I felt embarrassed and overwhelmed with frustration, not knowing what to do and who to talk to since I was staying alone. After trying hard to overcome my strange feelings, I quit NIE and kept to myself at home."

The weird feelings did not stop. She felt that people could read her mind and were playing matchmaking games with her. "I even thought that

PM Lee Kuan Yew [the Prime Minister of Singapore at the time] was trying to matchmake me. Everyone I saw on TV and listened to in the radio were talking to me directly and personally. If I did not comply to their wishes, I was sure they would treat me very harshly. I felt confused and overwhelmed. I tried to bring myself back to reality but it was impossible. I heard voices and was delusional."

Jailed for throwing killer litter

Her schizophrenia was so acute that she was charged in court for throwing killer litter. "I was so frustrated, and looked out of my window. I felt so angry that I began to throw things out. I threw my standing mirror, my chili pounder. I cannot remember what else I threw out, but it was categorized as killer litter. I looked out the window again and what I saw was devastating. So many people were watching and challenging me to throw more things. I even felt that they were challenging me to jump down."

Soon after that, the police broke into her house and arrested her and sent her to the police station, then to the Institute of Mental Health (IMH). At IMH, the doctor diagnosed her with schizophrenia, and she was warded for a month, before standing trial in court. "I was sentenced to one-week jail, which I served with much regret for my conduct, but really could not have helped it because I was not thinking clearly."

After that, she lived in denial of her illness and did not take her medicines because what she felt and saw seemed so real. She thought that everyone in Singapore could read her mind and they were planning to sabotage her every action. "I felt I had to leave Singapore for a fresh start away from all these mean people."

An American adventure

In 2000, Haslinah embarked on a journey to the United States of America (USA) with just a one-way flight ticket and USD$200. One month prior to the journey, she had secured a job with a Spanish family in California who agreed to pay her USD$200 per month plus food and lodging, in exchange for taking care of their one-year-old daughter.

It was an adventure that she would not have taken if not for her mental disorder. She was welcomed in Los Angeles by the Spanish family but after one month, they broke a promise. "I saw pork in their groceries even though they had agreed not to cook pork. I was upset and asked them why they lied to me. They said that it was no big deal, but it was a big deal to me. So, I took my backpack and left," Haslinah recalled.

She headed straight to the Malaysian Embassy in California where she thought she could find help from other Muslims. There, she found a beautiful Malaysian lady, Hanah, who housed and connected her to wealthy Muslims homes where she worked as an ad-hoc housekeeper and nanny.

But she could not help but think that others were reading her mind even though she appeared to be surviving well. "The truth is, I was running away from Singapore to get away from the people who were reading my mind, but it persisted all the way in California. I felt devastated and was living in tears and pain."

Finally, after 18 months in California, Hanah asked if she wanted to go home. She offered to help get her a ticket back home or instead work as a barista in New York. She declined the latter and reached home in September 2001. One week after her return, an airplane to New York crashed on September 11. "I was shocked but also relieved when I saw the news on TV. Allah loved me so much that He had saved me from that disaster. If I had chosen to go to New York, I could have been one of the passengers in the plane. Alhamdulillah, Allah is Great!"

No longer in denial

Upon returning to Singapore, she worked in another Islamic kindergarten but again left suddenly due to her illness. At the exit interview, she disclosed her illness and was referred to an in-house counsellor. "This counsellor opened my mind. Unlike the other doctors, she challenged me to research on my illness. I discovered that I was not alone. So many people also hear voices and are delusional, just like the professor in the movie, 'A Beautiful Mind'."

Heavenly match

There were times when friends tried to matchmake her to men, some of whom were ex-convicts and ex-drug addicts. She understood that Allah was testing her, but these efforts made her feel more hurt and unloved.

But one match turned out to be made in Heaven. She was introduced to a gem of a husband, Mohammed Nashedur Rahmaan, 54, a Bengali British, by one of her Qur'anic students. They were on an online chat group and when he asked her to find him a wife, she asked Haslinah if she would be interested. Her friend gave her telephone number to Nashedur Rahmaan and, not long after, they started chatting. After he performed the *umrah* (minor pilgrimage), he met her in Singapore in November 2010. After a week, she brought him to see her doctor in IMH and even made him pay for her medical bills. She said, "A few days later, I was surprised when he proposed to me. I asked him why me? He said, because I had been completely truthful to him about my weaknesses. He appreciated my honesty and I loved him even more."

On 6 February 2011, they were wedded and have been happily so for the past nine years. But their marriage is not without challenges. "We have been apart since the third year of our marriage. That is because his S-Pass was not approved by the Singapore government and so he had to return to UK to find a job for us to survive. At first, I was worried that he would forget about me once he left me since that happened to many other women. However, to my surprise and relief, until today he still stands by my side."

When Nashedur Rahmaan first started a new life in UK, he earned only 400 pounds, yet he still sent her half of it as her *nafaqah* (maintenance). "Alhamdulillah, I am grateful to Allah for his generosity and unlimited love for me. Now I believe what the Qur'an says that after every difficulty there will be ease. I had been suffering for nearly 20 years and now I was being loved unconditionally without him even considering my plain and obese look."

Speaking fondly of her husband, Haslinah said, "He is naturally a very gentle soul. His kind heart and understanding helped me to recover and learn to be a better person. His wisdom taught me a lot about life and its challenges. Every day he never fails to call me early in the morning and at lunch time to check if I am OK."

Healing slowly but surely

However, resilient as she is, Haslinah can still be triggered and suffer from relapses although they are less frequent. Since her first hospitalisation at the age of 27, she has occasionally been in and out the hospital because of relapses. Usually, her triggers are reminders of her heartbreak or of the injustices she went through in her younger years.

"I think I am fairly recovering now because I am at the stage where I know when I am relapsing and will turn to the doctor for advice should it happen. I seldom get hospitalised unless I really feel depressed and need to recuperate in a safe environment. I used to feel suicidal, however, after my marriage, I feel that I am living for more than just myself. I have a loved one whom I do not want to disappoint. I do not want to break his heart by doing anything silly."

Yet, she is still on the road to healing and recovering her true self even as she is dealing with her paranoia and even as people are judging her. But she is grateful that at least one pain has healed thanks to the unconditional love of her spouse.

When she was young, Haslinah was hardworking but, nowadays, because of her mood swings, she is only able to work during her upbeat mood and sleeps all day during her downside mood. "My moods go up and down and sometimes I cannot figure what my triggers are," she says ruefully.

A dream comes true

However, throughout her work experience with her interrupted careers as a kindergarten teacher and an IT trainer, she has achieved her dream to be an Islamic children's book author.

A freelance Quran-reading teacher to young children now, her passion has always been working with kids. Feeling there was a gap in stories in English to share the nature of Allah, she thought of creating a book series on the 99 Beautiful Names of Allah. So far, she has finished two books *Asmaaullaahil Husnaa Short Stories* vols 1 and 2. "In each book, I write about 11 names of Allah for our children to read and understand their meanings in the form of colourful stories. In this journey, I have learnt so much more about Allah through His 99 Attributes and learnt to turn to Him more in times of hardships."

Patience and forgiveness

Her life's journey is not only about being patient but learning to forgive and let Allah do what is best for her. "Forgiving was difficult for me because I was boiled up with anger and frustration at many people around me, especially my close relatives. I felt that my siblings did not know or understand my illness and my struggles. Initially, I was always fighting and arguing with them."

However, as time went by, she learnt from Club HEAL's sessions to let go. "As I learnt to let go of my anger, I began to see my siblings' support for me throughout my illness. I felt that they may have contributed to my illness, but they also have contributed to my recovery. It is fair enough to say that there is justice after all, but before that I was too blinded by my own anger and frustrations."

She also learnt from a book to let Allah do what was best for her. So began a journey to forgive and build positive relationships with love and care. This mindset changed her life as she became much more contented and happier. "When I stayed with my nephew and niece, they appealed to me not to throw tantrums in front of their children. My heart melted to see the children and I became less angry. There, I learnt to re-love my family and they reciprocated my love. I learnt to be humble enough to listen to their scolding. Even though I felt they were unjust, I still listened without anger. I feel I have gradually become a more beautiful soul, day after day."

Alone but not lonely in a beautiful sanctuary

Presently, Haslinah is staying at home alone in a 2-room HDB flat purchased for her by her husband. At first, it was hard for her to stay at home alone again as she had been doing this since a little girl. However, as she read more books and listened to more Islamic lectures, she learnt to be more grateful with what she had. "Now, even though I am alone, deep inside I am not in pain anymore because I have a loving and understanding husband who calls me twice a day. In fact, I am so grateful that he did not ditch me when he returned to the UK. Alhamdulillah, I thank Allah that He gave me beautiful love after he tested me with pain and sorrows. Thank you, Allah for my marital home, this beautiful sanctuary that you have gifted me with. I have learnt to count my blessings and be thankful for everything that I have."

Yet, at first, it was difficult to feel gratitude when she was afflicted with this illness. She thought Allah hated her and was punishing her. "But Allah did not mean to hate or punish me. He was shaping my soul to be a beautiful one. Just like the chisel's rough edge – when it is sharpened it will be just as smooth as the other edge," she asserted philosophically.

The promise of Allah: with every hardship there will be ease

My struggle to be grateful began when my heart was broken during my first exposure to love. I felt that Allah has taken away my parental love and later Allah was taking away my first love from my heart and causing me great pain. How could I be grateful to Allah? Amidst it all, the people surrounding me did not help much to soothe the pain."

Haslinah confided that there was a time when she stopped praying and reading the Quran due to her anger at God until He sent her a reminder. "One night, when in bed, I felt that I was approaching death. I was terribly scared of my sins. I got up and tried to pray, trembling with fear. I looked around for a Quran but shockingly there were none to be found. I cried and cried on my prayer mat. There and then, I realized that Allah had given me a chance to redeem my sins. I was grateful to Him for allowing me to repent to Him, and since then, I have never let go of the Quran. I began to teach the Holy Book to anybody who was interested, especially to the young," she added.

"I have learnt to be grateful for every little thing that I have and to rebuild my relationship with Allah. I have learnt to give to charity even when I have barely enough for myself. I have learnt to be humble even in the face of injustice. I have learnt to accept others, even with their shortcomings. I have learnt to trust Allah, especially during calamities. After every hardship, there *will* be ease. If we keep believing in Him and are thankful to Him, He will give us *more* than what we ask for. This is His *promise* to us," she adds emphatically.

And that was how she received the happy ending Allah promises for the patient and the grateful.

5

MY JOURNEY

My name is Kate Loreto, I am 45 years old and I am a Senior Peer Support Specialist at Singapore Association for Mental Health (SAMH)'s Oasis Day Centre. I have been living with mental illness for 23 years now and this is my recovery story.

Death wish

For many years in mental distress, my fear of God's punishment prevented me from actively attempting suicide. I slept a lot, praying to God to let me die in my sleep. My active studying of self-help books created positivity within me when I was not busy praying for my death. This went on for 13 years until I finally found the courage to seek help.

I was diagnosed with major depressive disorder in October 2010 and generalized anxiety disorder in December 2015. However, looking back, I had my first symptoms of depression as early as October 1997, following two traumatic events within that same year. Both events changed the way I saw myself and others. My self-esteem and self-confidence had been destroyed.

Self-help

At that time, no one was there to help me spot my distorted perceptions and false beliefs. The fear of stigma and cost of treatment prevented me from seeking professional help. Instead, I turned to religion by reading the scriptures and serving in church. I also pored over self-help books. When I needed to talk, I turned to one supportive friend who always gave a listening ear.

Healing versus cure

I have learnt that healing and cure are two different things. To quote Dr Jon Kabat-Zinn, healing is about *relating differently* to what has hurt us, be it a traumatic event, an illness, or a disability. It is about coming to terms with things as they are, while cure is almost always about getting rid of the symptoms of an illness.

With mental illness, healing plays a more important role in the recovery journey as there is currently no cure for mental illness. The medications we take only suppress the symptoms and once we stop taking the medications, the symptoms will surface again. Healing our wounded minds through various forms of psychological therapies is a must if we want to improve our wellness.

I like the definition of recovery used by the Substance Abuse and Mental Health Services in the US:

Recovery is a process of change through which individuals improve their health and wellness, live a self-directed life, and strive to reach their full potential.

This definition focuses on who I can be regardless of mental illness. It also highlights that I need to take charge of my decisions and to make changes to improve my situation. It means that I can still be experiencing symptoms of mental illness but that will not stop me from taking charge and work towards getting back on my feet and achieving my dreams.

The stages of recovery

In the first Peer Support Specialist course that I attended in September 2013, we learnt that there are five stages of recovery:

1. Impact of illness

This is the stage when the symptoms of mental illness are active and the person experiencing them cannot function. At this point, medical intervention is needed to suppress or reduce the symptoms and restore the person's functioning.

2. Life is limited

But medications cannot heal the trauma experienced by the person caused by the symptoms of mental illness. Because of that traumatic experience, the person starts to believe that he is limited because he has mental illness. A person can be in this stage for years until he experiences something that challenges that belief and moves on to the stage where he starts to believe that change is possible.

3. Change is possible

This is the stage where the person starts to think hopefully, "maybe it is possible for me to have a good life even if I have mental illness".

4. Commitment to change

With external support fueling the fire of hope within the person, he starts to make the necessary commitment for his recovery.

5. Actions for change

Commitment needs to be supported by action. This is the stage where the person continually does the things needed for his recovery.

It is important to note that it is still possible for relapses to happen in each stage of recovery and it is also possible to move from one stage to another in a non-linear manner. Currently, I am in stage 5, yet because of a severe relapse that may possibly happen in the future, my belief in myself and in recovery may crumble and I will regress to stage 2. But with the help of a skilled therapist, I will remember my strengths and dreams, and will bounce back straight to stage 5 again.

Stigma

Another issue to note is that aside from symptoms, external and self-stigma makes mental illness debilitating. Medications cannot address stigma. Acceptance will address external stigma while psychological therapies will address self-stigma.

We can never have total control over how other people think of us; we have, however, full control over how we see ourselves. It is vital that we maximize that control by working with skilled therapists who can help us identify our blind spots when it comes to seeing ourselves objectively and compassionately.

Walking the path patiently

Patience does not come naturally to me. But if there is something that recovering from mental illness has taught me, it is patience.

Recovery takes a long time. In fact, recovery will take a lifetime, if we look at the definition I mentioned earlier. We will only know if we have lived to our fullest potential at the end of our lives.

There is also the issue of relapses. Sometimes, even with our best efforts to stay well, the mental illness sets in and relapses still happen.

*Im*patience, I have learnt, is one of the fastest ways to damage our mental health. If we can see that recovery is a continuous learning experience rather than a one-time event or destination for us to reach after a certain time, we will sit back, relax and enjoy the ride. Patience then, will be natural, for no one can force learning. We will learn only when we are ready to learn. This is what I have noticed in other parts of my life when there is no pressure for me to perform.

Expressing gratitude is difficult

When I am experiencing depressive symptoms, being grateful is difficult. When I am experiencing anxiety symptoms, expressing gratitude triggers panic attacks. It is strange but true. Nevertheless, gratitude has played and still plays an important part in my healing.

While gratitude can be a tool for healing for some, for me it is the key indicator that healing has finally happened. I know I am healed when I can look back at an event that had caused me so much pain and suffering and see its gifts with gratitude. It is like looking at a beautiful lotus flower that has blossomed out of a muddy pond.

I now make it a point to seek out precious gifts that are buried in painful experiences that I have gone through. Seeing them takes out the unnecessary suffering from the pain and it makes the experience worthwhile.

Mindfulness helps

I have always been interested to learn meditation since I was in university. But I was not interested to learn Buddhism. I am grateful for an old friend who introduced me to Brahm Centre in 2012 to learn mindfulness. I did not understand much of what was taught then. In 2014, I took up Mindfulness- Based Cognitive Therapy at Khoo Teck Puat Hospital. This time, it was a bit better – I understood about breathing. Learning how to breathe helped me tide over the difficult periods during panic attacks and relapses. But there is more to mindfulness than just breathing. So, in 2018, I decided to learn mindfulness once again. I went back to Brahm Centre and to date, I have attended a total of seven courses, inclusive of retreats. Currently, I am attending my eighth course.

Mindfulness has changed my life. I am still not an expert on it although my knowledge and skills have improved since 2012. Learning and practicing mindfulness has helped heal my mind and has also equipped me with skills to cope with intense and powerful emotions in a way that will not destroy me.

My career in mental health services

In 2012, SAMH trained and hired its first Peer Support Specialist. A Peer Support Specialist is someone who has first-hand experience with mental illness and recovery. He is trained and certified to provide peer support services in the following ways: (a) as a role model of recovery; (b) as an advocate that recovery is real; (c) as a support to fellow Persons In Recovery by providing one-on-one peer support and facilitating recovery-oriented programmes; and (d) as a support to fellow colleagues by providing insights on the recovery process using his lived experiences.

I am grateful that SAMH brought in Peer Support Specialists to be a part of its mental health ecosystem. On top of adding value to the services of the organization, it was lifesaving for me too. For once, I had a chance to leverage on an experience that I thought was a liability. And that experience comprised a big part of my life. I am grateful to have good use for it. This Peer Support Specialist experience has challenged the stigma I have due to my living with mental illness. I am still in the early stages of setting out a career for myself. That is another mountain for me to climb.

Keep going on

Healing and recovery take a long time and require active effort on our part. No one can walk the path for us, no matter how much our loved ones want to do so. But there are many people out there who are willing to walk this journey with us. Some will accompany us till the end, some a few steps, some halfway, it does not matter. What matters is that we are loved and valued beyond our wildest imagination.

6

A TWIN PROBLEM, A MULTIPLE DELIGHT

Bringing a pair of twins into this world is never an easy labour. For Nur Marina Abdullah Chong, 38, Manager of Fund Development and Communications at Club HEAL, it was a frightening fight for the lives of Ehsan and Elyas, now healthy boys in Primary One.

The twins were delivered via emergency caesarean-section when Ehsan's water bag burst at the 24th week of her pregnancy. Marina had not expected them to be carried to full term as, generally, the chance of this happening for twins is slim, but she was still not prepared to give birth so early.

A battle to survive

Their delivery and early days were among the most difficult moments in her life. At birth, the babies were tiny – 670 g and 805 g respectively.

Marina and her husband, Shahrin Latif, 42, manager at another social service sector, were worried that their precious ones would not survive.

Marina recalled, "Lying there on the bed hearing doctors and nurses telling you about all sorts of complications that the twins might face was not easy. It was scary and the thought of losing one of them was worse. At 24 weeks-old, they might not even have their eyes developed properly. Mentally, my husband and I were drained. Physically, I was weak and in lots of pain. I remembered praying very hard. I told God, "You have blessed us with this pair, and it is up to You whether You let them survive."

"In fact, Ehsan almost died when he was a week old. With God's blessing, the doctors and nurses managed to bring him back to safety," Marina shared. The couple knew their lives had changed forever and they had a different route to take. "The learning journey for pre-term twins was going to be different but we told ourselves it was okay to be different," said Marina, who has another boy, Kaysan, 9, who was also delivered pre-term at 34 weeks. In June 2019, she gave birth to Nur Khayrah at 35 weeks. She was in labour for an agonising five days.

A playful pair through multiple support

Seven years down the road, the twins are boisterous boys like most of their peers. "They are healthy and playful. And we are thankful to those who have walked with us and supported us during those scary times." Her mum has always been the pillar for their special family, with the help of their first helper, Jannah. "They looked after the children until they were all off to childcare. And my husband's parents helped by sending the children for check-ups and bring them out for walks."

Dealing with depression

Marina who had suffered from depression, gave up her career the moment she found that she was pregnant again, after suffering a prior miscarriage. For three years after giving birth also, she only took on part-time jobs just to have more time with her babies. She wanted to be in the best state of mental health to carry her children in her pregnancy and to take care of them. In her younger years, before her marriage, she confesses she had made a few suicide attempts and "*not* because of BGR (Boy-Girl-Relationships)".

Marina explained, "I was under a lot of stress as I was the sole breadwinner after my father's sudden death. I was 24 years old and had just started working. My mum was retired, and my brother was in National Service. Being the eldest child, I felt responsible and wanted to shoulder everything, so things got tough. It hit me quite hard. Having to deal with my mum who was going through the sudden loss of my father, and menopause too, was challenging. It was a journey to hell and back."

Anxiety attacks

She developed anxiety disorder while working at a company prior to Club HEAL. She had to manage three portfolios with high key performance indices and felt responsible for her team. "For about a year, I kept waking up in cold sweat and having panic attacks." In June 2018, she succumbed to a mild stroke and decided to throw in the towel.

"My health and family were definitely more important," she said. "It was great to concentrate on my growing family with Shahrin. I have always been good with children. Therefore, it helped when we had our own. Coping with three boys who are very close, age-wise, was not easy. But we managed, with lots of love."

A journey of patience and gratitude

Healing from her trauma – physical, mental, and emotional – is a journey she is still on. She suffers from panic attacks at times. "Whenever, I have my anxiety attack, I will sit up and breathe. I tell myself to be patient and wait. It is okay to be not okay."

This jovial lady who always lights up the room with her warmth, says, 'I have a positive mindset, and I believe nothing is impossible if your heart and intention are in the right place." Her optimism helped her tide through her challenges. That, and a spirit of gratitude. "I learned to say Thank You and hug people around me during those difficult times."

A vocation of sharing

To Marina, healing is more about the physical recovery. "Emotionally and mentally, I am always recovering. Sharing of experience helps in this. Till today, I am still sharing my stories to parents who are going through the same journey as I did," she said.

Since working in Club HEAL from December 2018, she has been able to help those with mental health issues face up to their challenges with her compassion and humour. "Working at Club HEAL has made me realise that not being well is not the end. With love and support, our journey in life can get better. Being thankful helps me be contented with life. I contribute by sharing with people around me that having mental health illness is not *malu* (shameful). Recovery is possible."

7

CONSTANT PAIN, MY CONSTANT COMPANION

I am Roszita bte Idrus, 54 years old. I have Fibromyalgia Syndrome (FMS). Before FMS, I was also diagnosed with anxiety and have experienced depression. Up till today, I do not know what the cause of all this pain is. Even before 2009, when I was diagnosed first as having chronic muscle pain, I had gone to private clinics and they all told me, "It is just muscle pain, or perhaps stress." There are many symptoms of FMS, like experiencing migraines, tightness of muscles in the neck which are so tight at times, I cannot even turn my head for a few days, and my veins in my head will appear after hurting so bad, like having an extreme toothache. My veins are so tight it feels like they might rupture. My muscles feel like they are being stabbed with a knife. My nerves feel like they are being poked with needles.

Tortured daily

I cannot leave the house because the heat and brightness of the sun feels torturous to me. I also experience 'brain fog', a dreamy state, where it is difficult for me to concentrate. My right hip also feels painful and the ache shoots to my legs. Sometimes, when I walk, I fall suddenly. It feels like I have a cancer that has spread over my whole body. At times, I imagine there is an alien inside me, gnawing at my bones. I hear a constant buzzing in my ears, and I am sensitive to sounds. I have even lost my sense of taste and smell, although not totally. I have not had a good rest or good sleep for almost 30 years. Even when I sleep, my muscles and nerves do not seem to relax.

Triggers are many for me. It could be when doing house chores as the strain for it would cause me pain, even going out and returning my body would ache badly. I panic easily if something happens and thus, this will make my nerves and muscles very tight.

Lonely, yet staying grateful

I am currently unemployed and divorced with two kids. My daughter, 35, is married and my son, 33, is single. Yet I live on my own and I struggle and cope alone. I believe I am a difficult person to live with. Someone once said to me, to "just go with the flow". Trust me, I want to, but something prevents me from doing so. I feel like I do not know how to show love. My mom used to be very supportive, but she is old now and has dementia. She has always believed in me. My siblings, however, do not believe I am unwell because I look normal. They think that perhaps it is all in my head and there is nothing really wrong with me – that I am making excuses about my condition. I do not blame them for thinking this; it is indeed difficult to understand what I am going through.

To survive, I try my best to divert my attention to something positive. If I do not do this, going through each second is a momentous struggle. The COVID-19 pandemic has been especially challenging: I could not go for my psychologist appointments, see my doctor, or attend counselling sessions during the Circuit Breaker period. I could not go for the rehab sessions in Club HEAL. And my pain seemed worse. Thankfully, it coincided with the blessed month of Ramadan, so I tried to focus on my fasting to divert my attention from my difficulties. When I felt isolated, I thought about the people who have been supporting me in the health care sector, such as my counsellor, psychologist and doctor; my friends and staff at Club HEAL; and especially my daughter and son-in-law. They already have so much on their shoulders, so I resolved to take care of myself mentally to reduce the load on everyone else as we went through the pandemic together. I remain very grateful for the support I have from them.

No cure, but coping

I do not think I am in healing or recovery yet. To me, healing means reaching a stage where I can do so much more without feeling so much pain or when I can sleep soundly and getting up would not feel like I have been beaten up while sleeping. Recovery means I can always live without extreme fear and feeling like wanting to run away.

There is no cure for FMS, but I have learnt to live with it. Coping means being forced to swim throughout the day and managing only to keep my head above the water, so that I do not drown. My coping mechanism is to practise endurance. To overcome my challenges, to be grateful, I have stopped asking "WHY?" I believe that He has put me here for a reason. So, I accept my condition, and focus on trying to get better.

Share and reach out

I share with very, very few people about my condition. I prefer to listen to others rather than to explain my condition. It is hard to find a support group in Singapore for FMS, so do try to talk to someone who is willing to listen patiently, even if they do not really understand, just talk about it so as to create awareness someday. For fellow sufferers of FMS, find out more about the illness online, do research and listen to people who have gone through similar experiences.

I feel relieved that I am not alone – what I am going through is real and not just in my head, like people have suggested to me. I am not making it up. Reach out!

8

HEALING BY LETTING GO

My name is Sarinah Said, 49, and I have been a Programme Executive at Club HEAL for two years. This is my story of Healing from depression, which I had experienced since childhood due to some losses I had suffered. I carried on despite the struggles and did not express my feelings. Later, I was diagnosed with Post-Natal Depression in 2000, and in 2004. I did not seek treatment as my family and I thought we could manage. This culminated in a diagnosis of Major Depressive Disorder (MDD) in 2013.

In 2017, my Club HEAL journey began. I believe the lessons I have learned in this path, especially in letting go of the past, will benefit others in their own journey of healing and recovery. Initially, it was tough for me to accept the truth that I was suffering from a mental health condition. I did not have anyone to help me understand the pain I was going through. I had to fend for myself and find ways to get help. Now, I can finally say I have healed. Finally, yes! I did it!

Searching for truth

I am now able to understand the importance of letting go of things which are not worth holding on to. I want to be happy and cherish the time I have with those who need support in their recovery journeys. I will search for my own truth and allow others to do the same. I will value my own vision and others' too. I know each of us are on our own paths, making the decisions that are right for us.

My lived experience, my strength

I found my strength in helping people with mental health challenges through my own experiences. I know life is not easy for people like us and that we need the support of our loved ones. Unfortunately, it may not be easy to make them understand our feelings and struggles. We go through anxiety, trauma, paranoia, psychosis, depression, hearing voices, suicidal thoughts, *etc*. As our caregivers and friends are not mental health professionals, it is understandable that they do not know how to support us. But there are many resources available to aid us – through various organisations – in this healing journey.

Live and let go

I hope when you get support from these places, you can live in the "here and now" and allow life to happen instead of trying to force outcomes. Only when you relinquish regrets about the past and fears about the future, you can truly make the most of each present day.

I am thankful to have found out where to look for help and find the strength to never give up. Through my psychiatrist Prof Dr Joseph Leong, I got to know of Club HEAL – the place where my recovery journey began.

The beautiful characters at Club HEAL

I was assigned to a counsellor, Ms Balqis, a sweet and humble woman who motivated me immensely. She encouraged me to attend rehab at the Club. Finding out that I was not alone and making new friends (including the elderly) at rehab, made me happy; we were like a family. I accepted their love, which I had been longing for ever since I lost someone close to me.

I found rehab activities meaningful to my present life. One of my favourite sessions was the Motivational Talk by Mr Zainal, who is now my Rehab Manager. His talks really touched me and give me the confidence to keep going on.

There is a volunteer, Ms Sharifah, who shared about mindfulness and helped me understand the word 'Forgiveness'. I learnt that when forgiving, I had to be clear and positive about what I was forgiving and take responsibility for my own actions. I will seek Allah's help to clarify why I need to apologize and do so without reservations.

A staff at Club HEAL who believes in me and constantly gives me encouragement is Ms Sumaiyah. She is currently the Programme Coordinator of a programme called "Our Healing Voice" or OHV. It is a powerful programme to help a person-in-recovery gain self-confidence and contribute to society.

At Club HEAL, I was excited to find someone who is good at pottery, Mdm Junainah or Kak Junn. I had long wanted to try my hand at this craft, and she helps peers to do pottery as part of the healing process. She herself is a peer with a remarkable recovery story. Kak Junn is our Rehab Programme Coordinator and she recommended me to be a Programme Executive. I feel happy that I have been given this compliment, trust, and gift. It reaffirms that I am deserving of good things, so I will simply say, "Thank You".

Kak Junn encouraged me to attend the "Peer Support Specialist" (PSS) course conducted by the National Council of Social Services (NCSS).

Changing course

The PSS course changed my life. It helped me put into perspective all the nightmare of pain and emotions that I had gone through. There, I met peers with mental illness who suffered greater pain. We heard each other's stories; learnt from each other; and vowed to inspire others like us one day, removing their fear, loneliness, and hopelessness. But change must start from ourselves.

Being the true me

I have learnt to affirm that my knowledge, feelings, and beliefs are just as valid as anyone else's. I am open to learning from others and their experiences, but I will stand my ground firmly. I will honour, cherish, and love myself. When I get confused about what to do, I now remind myself that I need to be true to myself. I will break free from others' expectations of me.

Yesterday is over

Today, I am direct, clear, and honest in my dealings with other people. I am comfortable with myself and others can sense it. When I make a mistake, I realize that it is only part of the learning process. Old, negative patterns of thinking no longer limit me. I let them go with ease and each day is a new opportunity for me. Yesterday is over and done. The greatest gift I can give to myself is "Unconditional Love". I love myself exactly as I am. I no longer wait to be perfect before I love myself. I learn to release all resistance to expressing my creativity fully, as ideas come to me easily and effortlessly.

Valuable lessons

I trust that the events in my life are not random. My experiences are not mistakes, and God is not angry with me. I have gone through and am going through exactly what I need to learn something valuable, something that will prepare me for the joy and love I am seeking.

Grateful for a wonderful workspace

My workspace is a pleasure to be in. There is mutual respect among my colleagues. My job allows me to express my talents and abilities, and I am grateful. Here, it is safe to speak up for myself and stand on my own two feet and use my strength and power. I can create easily and effortlessly when I let my thoughts come from the loving space of my own heart. I believe my support system is strong and loving. Everyone has my best interests at heart. When I encounter problems in my job, I am willing to ask for help. Limitations are merely opportunities to grow. I use them as stepping-stones to success.

Acceptance and love

Now I always wake up in the morning and take a deep breath to start a good day. I plan everything to be as good as I feel. My anticipation attracts good experiences to me. I feel everyone in my life has something to teach me. We have a purpose in being together.

I have come to the end of my sharing about letting go and moving forward with strength. I hope it helps you create joy in every area of your life. We all can experience wealth, health, self-esteem, job success, creativity and a life released from resentment and pain. When you accept all parts of yourself, you heal.

Thank you, Club HEAL, for accepting me as one of you.

9

TURNING AFFLICTION TO ADVOCACY

Nur Afiqah bte Mohd Azman, 28, graduated with a degree in Biological Science from the Nanyang Technological University in 2016 but her affliction with Schizoaffective Disorder changed her career direction and mission in life. Now, Afiqah has embarked on a promising career in the mental health sector as an intern at Club HEAL.

It was loneliness at the university that lead to her first meltdown in 2018. "I had a hard time making friends. People whom I used to know drifted away. I was worried about not having friends to the point that I simply I broke down."

The haunting

This young lady with a sweet and serene demeanour could not sleep and started hearing voices. Her mood swung up and down. She recalled,

"It was scary. I felt like someone was following me wherever I went."

Although she was hospitalised at NUH Psychiatric Ward for about a month in February 2018, she was only officially diagnosed in January 2019. "I thought people were talking bad about me and laughing at me – even the TV news was disparaging me. This delusion is known as 'Idea of Reference'," she shared.

The confirmation from her doctor that she was suffering from a serious mood disorder created fear and worry about her future. Afiqah said, "I was distressed when I got to know that I was mentally ill. I was afraid that it would be hard for me to be employed."

Jobs related to her degree were not easy to come by. Afiqah worked as a relief teacher, teaching numerous subjects for a year in a primary school. "It was a great platform for me to gain confidence to talk to a lot of people," she reflected. Her confidence to accept herself and her illness grew when she became a client at Club HEAL in 2019, seeking counselling and rehabilitation. With her passion for writing, she is now a regular contributor of poems to the Club's MentallyBlessed.blog. Her creativity, positive attitude, kindness, and abilities did not go unnoticed.

Afiqah the Advocate

Being with Club HEAL also instilled a sense of urgency to educate others about mental illness although she has never personally experienced stigma. So, when she was invited to be the poster girl for the Beyond the Label movement with Resilience Collective to gain acceptance for people with mental disorders, she leapt at the opportunity to help change society's mindsets.

This led to further doors for advocacy opening. "I have just been accepted to be an intern at Club HEAL for nine months. I would like to work towards a career as a peer support specialist in the mental health field." As a peer support specialist, she will support people with mental disabilities cope with their conditions and recover through her own lived experience with mental health challenges.

Person in recovery

Right now, she is in the early stage of recovery. She had a relapse recently on 13 April 2020. "The triggers were mainly overthinking and stressing myself out over what other people thought of me. I was provoked by an argument with one of my family members. I really wanted to be hospitalised as I always felt unsafe even though I was not abused at all. I did not feel safe with myself and my surroundings. Being hospitalised gave me some space, to take a breather."

She is thankful that her family, especially her parents, have been concerned about her well-being from the beginning and are very supportive of her recovery till now. Being thankful to them helps in the healing process. She said, "During my recent relapse, I tried my best to be grateful for my family, for the roof over my head and for the clothes I get to wear each day. I am truly grateful that I have everything that I need."

Persevere patiently

Gratitude is fortified by patience. "Patience contributes to my journey of wellness. With patience, it becomes easier for me to get through the day no matter how tough it is. Otherwise, I might be too distressed to complete my tasks or to work on my healing."

Afiqah notes that healing is not the same as recovery. "I see healing as the inner work we do on ourselves, such as inculcating self-love, gratitude, forgiveness. And I see recovery as being able to function properly and cope with my symptoms."

"Healing differs from one person to other. We cannot force anyone to heal. Healing starts from within. Healing needs to start first from within, then recovery follows. Healing is important because we need to do a lot of inner workings on ourselves in order to recover," Afiqah reflected.

Afiqah's hobbies, one of which is photography, helps her heal and recover. "I love taking portraits of my friends in a creative environment or in nature. I write to cope with my illness and to express my thoughts and feelings." She records her photography, poems and reflections on her website at https://nurafiqahbtemohdaz.wixsite.com/site.

Time heals

"My advice to my peers is that healing takes time and we cannot expect to heal within a few days. It might take months, even years. Everyone is in charge of their own healing and has to do it at their own pace."

Like many who walk her path, she is grateful for the insights the illness has given her about her strengths and weaknesses.

"Most people do not realise that mental illness is a gift that helps us become more attuned to our emotions and feelings, feelings that we sometimes ignore to please others."

Healing
By Nur Afiqah bte Mohd Azman

As the physical being needs healing,
As the spiritual being needs healing,
Our emotional being needs it too;
It is like a transparent silk draping around you,
controlling how you feel, how you think, how you behave.

Healing itself needs time and effort,
Done with courage and resilience,
Planted with hope and gratitude.

Healing is not linear,
It moves forward and backward,
Forward and backward,
Till it shows a sign of stability.

Emotional healing,
Forgiveness to self,
Forgiveness to others,
Seeks tremendous amount of self-love,
A battle worse than a battlefield,
A battle not seen by many,
A battle only the heart feels.

With self-love comes healing,
With hope comes healing,
With gratitude comes healing,
With forgiveness comes healing,
It is like a different coloured transparent
silk draping around you,
That soothes your soul with ease.

Healing can't be done in isolation,
Healing needs me, you and them.

When you follow your bliss,
You follow your inner compass,
You are moulded into something better,
Better than your past self.

Pain and suffering,
Pain and suffering shape you,
Shape you into something better,
Better for the present,
Your future self will thank you for that.

Thank you for keeping true to yourself,
To never fake a smile,
To never fake an intention,
To never fake the truth.

Dear self,
Thank you.
Thank you.
Thank you for seeking the path of healing.

10

THE ROAD TO REDISCOVERY

Most people think of recovery as a destination but for Ella Mohd, life is not about recovering but about rediscovering. She does not aim to "Recover" but always to "Rediscover". The glamourous, humorous, and boisterous cabin crew embraces life as an exciting and romantic adventure to discover new depths to herself. Each chapter of the journey leads to the next and reflects the evolution of her thoughts, ideas and principles and way of life.

For Ella, 36, every stage of her life has been a process of awakening. For instance, the early years of her adult life was a traumatic stage that she had to undergo to be the person she is today. Then, Ella suffered the symptoms related to depression. "I suffered from severe emotional distress when I was involved in an abusive relationship in my early 20's. I was not diagnosed with a mental illness and I was unsure how to label it." She did not seek treatment as her routine life gave her a sense of normalcy. "I felt that I was strong enough to overcome what I was going through on my own and that it was only temporary," she said.

In the pit of ill-health

Then, she experienced weight fluctuations due to irregular bowel movements, severe and extended bronchitis attacks triggered by high levels of stress, negative thoughts, and paranoia. "I felt frequently like a prisoner trapped by my own decisions. I had a lot of negative self-talk and constantly doubted myself. I would cry in a corner and chew my hair after episodes of emotional abuse," she recalled.

The man behind her ill health was none other than her own husband - someone who was supposed to be her protector but instead became her tormentor.

"On our wedding day, as we were leaving home to go to the hotel, he reminded me how useless I was and that he regretted marrying me. One week after that, he said, 'Your father has no say about you anymore, HAHA! You are under my rules now.'

"His laugh and the look on his face confirmed that he had plans to make sure my life was a living hell. I was shocked by these words. It was a 360-degree change. It was like he had been plotting this trap for the longest time. I realised that all his loving gestures before marriage was just a lure."

Although he did not physically abuse Ella, he used emotional blackmail to mentally disengage her from her emotions and way of life and tried to alter her views through negative reinforcement. "After several years of manipulation, I was 'trained' to accept a new normal. *His* normal," she continued.

He triggered Ella in many ways. "Every hurtful word of hate and disgust that was thrown at me to remind me I was useless and unworthy would trigger deep hurt and disturbing emotions, sometimes even suicidal thoughts. During arguments or misunderstandings, he would call me 'stupid', 'lazy,' 'disgraceful', and say 'no one cares for you,' 'everyone lies to you'. He would question my integrity and manipulate what I knew as the truth to be a lie. And he would build on a lie and make it look like the truth just to confuse me so that I would give in or give up after doubting myself and my reality. He used religion to threaten me and shame to expose what we did before marriage. I became fearful of living and wanted to end my life to end the pain."

She did end the pain, by ending the marriage in 2014. Ella summoned the courage to do this after learning about the roles of husbands and wives at an Islamic education centre. "After two years of *istikharah* prayers I finally was sure that the answer from God was to go ahead with the divorce." With this closure of the chapter of her life, Ella began the journey to healing. "Healing is a continuous process of always improving and maintaining a good state of mind and health, which is a path I am now always on. I enjoy finding new healing methods that work," she said.

No hate, no pain

While Ella no longer harboured hurt or pain, she did develop certain phobias because of the experience, including a fear of men who had similar features to her first husband. Four years after her divorce, however, she married Shan, 42. Ella speaks warmly of him. "We met on Facebook via a large network of our mutual friends. Following an innocent sharing of cat videos, he decided to say hello online. We chatted for a couple of hours and realised we had a lot of common interests. He asked me out for coffee and the rest is history."

The four years of healing earlier had prepared her for a new, healthy relationship. "This time, I was clear of what I would allow and not allow in my life; what kind of behaviour I could tolerate, and what I would not. He gave me freedom of speech and expression. His positive mindset was the characteristic that I was most attracted to. He was mature, pragmatic, and sensible and believed in mutual respect. He was very encouraging and assured me that I was capable of anything I dreamt of. This positive reinforcement helped me grow."

Bubbly babe

Ella has a great thing going for her – her infectious, bubbly spirit. "I would say I am a loving and positive person who finds joy in making people laugh. I love watching comedies like sitcoms or stand-up comedies. Laughing brings a healthy rush of endorphins. It makes my worries seem minor. I honed this skill to help me find comedy in tragedy. So, I retell the episodes I faced and highlight foolish acts. When I convey to people just how absurd some of my situations were – and they laugh – I feel better because I laugh with them."

Bigger problems abound

This ability to put things in perspective has put her in good stead. "Although I knew what I had been through was a horrible injustice, I knew there were many other cases far more traumatic than mine. I would sit in prayer and imagine looking down to earth from the stratosphere. I would see all the people who had no one left on this earth and how they were struggling every year celebrating Eid, hungry and desolate. I would imagine how some were chained in boxes or left for dead in the city with no money, no self-worth, and no opportunities. I would ask myself, 'How big is your problem compared to theirs?' I would burst into tears and seek forgiveness for thinking that I was lacking in life. Then, quietly, Gratitude would come and sit with me. Prayer and self-introspection have made me learn to appreciate what I have."

Keeping the faith

Spirituality has played an important part in her recovery. During her "relationship fiasco", she had attended Islamic classes for some time.

"These classes helped improve my knowledge on how to become a better Muslim and person, and to learn my rights as a woman and human being. Strengthening your faith is crucial to rediscovering yourself, hence recovering," Ella said.

Her mother helped her in this aspect. "My mother was a force to be reckoned with! She was very protective of her children, as most mothers are. She encouraged me through prayer and reinforced the importance of understanding and believing in God's ways and timing. She was my anchor."

Her siblings were too young to comprehend the seriousness of what she was going through at that time as she did not fully disclose to anyone her marital woes. "But my siblings have always been my source of laughter and light-heartedness. Being around them in a familiar environment made me feel safe and gave me a sense of belonging," Ella said.

Writing her way to sanity

A hobby that keeps her sane is writing. Going by her pen name LM, she would share her feelings or what she was going through in the form of poetries or short stories. "It was just a platform to dump all my negative emotions. I would post it online for other fellow poets in the community to read and critique. Some I posted publicly and some I kept private."

Today, she shares her day-to-day experiences and life's issues in a public blog with others on the road to recovery. She also heads a Meetup group in Singapore. The group meets monthly and is also for those in need of healing or a listening ear. Ella suggests trying different methods of healing. "You can't keep doing the same things and expect different results. If one method doesn't work, try another and another and another till you get a breakthrough."

Healing must always come to a full circle. It starts with the natural state of purity of mind, body and soul and should return to it. Said Ella, "If you don't see it in this light, you're going to be stuck in a vicious cycle of hate and pain."

Living
By LM

> *It Feels Like A Hundred Days -*
> *30 days and nights,*
> *Zombie land creeps into this already deformed nothingness*
> *Caught at the corner of my eye*
> *was the silent lamb of mystique beings ...*
> *I heard of them ... walking in the halls at night ...*
> *they roam this place like it was shared*
> *Like it was all prepared for viewing.*
> *An audience of one, I sit here again by my aching self ... contemplating Death.*
> *I suddenly thought of God, my ever so Loving Saviour.*
> *Then, pressed against me was the memories of the 'One'.*

I remembered what he meant to say, "What doesn't kill you makes you stronger?"
With each day that is how I've sketched my Life … in his very words …
just to survive this episode again, of Unforgiving Love.
There is no redemption to this, I will have to continue on, in this state of Mind …
Flawless are my words but not my face, hands or feet...
I have grown old, wrinkly and fat. Not for anyone to love …
But I don't pity myself … there's no begging for Love here … for I do not seek what is deemed impossible in my Lifetime …
Like the Immortal Lords of Love, the vampires, I have learned how to live alone in a crowded world.
A cold blanket of silence was suddenly brought upon me… I am alone again.
Whispers run pass me like fireflies in the dark, dragging my feet to my eternal bed, I plumped myself on the covers, crawled into sheets.
Insomnia seeps into my wake, intensely I feel "His" presence.
Everywhere I turn is just absolute emptiness, even when it's filled with materialistic things.
No cash or credit, car or condo can fill this void. I'd rather be with a poor man.
Not that the Master is not a poor man, he's just poor in sight and emotional conditions.
I wonder if Humans had the ability to fly … where would they dash off to?

The stars sit with me at the balcony usually, there aren't any tonight,
But I hope they'll come and visit me soon. I need the company.
I saw the Moon the other day, just a glance, she was awesome.
These 28 years in Human life, I've only come to learn now, what moves me,
makes me extremely Happy and what rocks my boat.
I've learned the type I fall for and know what activity I enjoy the most …
No … I'm not a hippie, or a wannabe musician,
The fact is clear, I can't do those things.
I love to write. But I lack inspiration where I come from.
However, one reason keeps me going … it is to know that someday …
I will be read, by persons who need me the most,
who need inspiration, who need motivation and clarity,
even though what I project is much confusion.
Some will get me. I have to be patient
Cause I'm looking forward to that someday…
Someday, Happiness will come my way, and when it does …
I want to embrace it with all my Heart and Soul …
and all the rays of the Sun … of the Matahari.

11

ABSENCE MADE THE MIND FLOUNDER

A lack of parental love from an absent father and a career-driven mother contributed to his Major Depressive Disorder. Derrick Looi Leong Kit, 28, Programme Executive at Club HEAL, was diagnosed with this mental condition at the tender age of 13.

He explained, "It was due to the lack of a father figure as my dad was stationed in China even before I was born. I only got to see him maybe once a year. I was also neglected by my mother as she was busy working to scale her career ladder. Also, my family members could not always get along, and I was caught in the middle. On top of that, there were stressors at school."

It was a lot on the plate for a teenager struggling to find his own identity and place in society. An introvert, he had his first relapse in 2013, while serving National Service. "I was admitted for one night in the general ward due to my suicidal thoughts but my mother had me discharged, due to her belief that I was not properly taken care of and would become worse if I were to remain in the ward."

Derrick's second relapse was in 2018. "It was due to school and the tension in the family was extremely high then," he recalled.

Triggering hope

A clear trigger for Derrick is quarrels with his girlfriend (now wife), Alody. "I met her at the polytechnic, and we started dating in 2010. We just got married in 2020." Although theirs is sometimes a tumultuous relationship, she is his main source of hope during recovery. Derrick shares, "As much as we have fought and quarreled throughout our relationship, she has never given up on me. She stood by me at the lowest point of my life and is very supportive, even though she is extremely against the use of medication."

Likewise, although they have their disagreements, his mother has been a key pillar in his life. "She has always been the one who supported me through my recovery. She raised me and is the one I look for when I face issues. She is also a source of my motivation to get better as I feel that it is only right for me to keep myself well for the sake of her peace of mind," Derrick said.

He confesses, further, to a love-hate relationship with his sister. "When we quarrel, we sometimes do not speak to each other for months. Nevertheless, when something crops up, we tend to go to each other for solace and comfort. It is an irreplaceable bond."

This is ironically the case with many peers: family is frequently the cause of mental health issues, but also the motivation for recovery. Family plays a large role in the healing process, which usually stems from wounds inflicted – often unwittingly – in childhood.

"Healing is the process to recovery – which means the absence of symptoms for a significant length of time. One cannot recover if one does not try to heal traumas, wounds, and past pain. Recovery is the end goal after struggling with mental illness. It is my personal belief that there is no cure for mental disorders, but one can recover through proper management and understanding oneself inside and out," said Derrick.

However, Derrick reckons his personality hampers his recovery. "I am very introverted and as such I require a lot of energy, emotionally, to engage with people. I tend to bottle up my emotions and find it difficult to share my problems, even with my wife."

The values he practices

Patience

Derrick feels that he needs to be patient with himself and especially with his expectations of recovery. "I need to learn from my mistakes and understand that certain things cannot be rushed, especially important life choices."

Gratitude

Being grateful is another key to his recovery. "It is a value my grandmother instilled in me since as far back as I can remember. She encouraged me to be grateful for everything that I have in my life. It helped me cope with my issues since I was young – such as the fact that my mother was never around due to her work. I reminded myself to be grateful that she was working so hard to ensure that my sister and I had the best of everything. Being grateful allowed me to appreciate the positives that I had in my life and not focus only on the negatives."

Sharing and caring

Having gone through the healing process, Derrick feels strongly about helping others in the same boat. "I relate my experiences through various media, including support group sessions. I do not shy away from my past and will openly share what I know or have been through with anyone who is interested."

And now, he can do this through his job at Club HEAL, where he had interned for over a year and officially started working as a Programme Executive since November 2019.

"I help peers at Club HEAL by mostly being present for them – they can come to me when they are feeling down. It is easier for them to communicate their feelings with me as I have similar experience. I also help by providing a different perspective to their issues. I support and empower those whom I work with, to better themselves and to better manage their conditions."

Unique position

Derrick is in a unique situation as a Chinese minority in a Malay/Muslim organization. The biggest issue for him is the language barrier as some peers are not fluent or even conversant in English, while he cannot speak much Malay. However, "working in Club HEAL has allowed me a chance to experience what being a 'minority' feels like. As a minority, even when they are not facing actual discrimination, there is a feeling of being outnumbered and fears that their concerns are unheard."

Understanding what it is like to be a minority is part of being a mental health advocate. Derrick does his part to remove stigma against people with mental illness. "I believe that everyone deserves the right to be mentally well, and that it is only possible when everyone accepts mental illness and do not see it as taboo anymore."

"We are moving towards that slowly and I hope that one day it will truly happen. We will be a society where people are not labelled by their illnesses and are seen for who they are and what they are meant to be."

12

MY PATH TO H.E.A.L.

Winning

By Sumaiyah Mohamed

> *Creatures, in my head, too long, cruel*
> *Invade uninvited and eat, grow ugly*
> *You are sloth-like, they say, big problem*
> *Chit-chatting brain never gives up*
>
> *The Amazon burns, and racism, enraged*
> *Tension, injustice and stillness*
> *I am cowered and quiet, mindless*
> *Am I asleep or is this a nightmare*
>
> *But, friends are lovely poetry lines*
> *And sunrise landscapes, a thousand*
> *tomorrows*
> *To treasure, thankful, thoughtful*
> *Do you know, angels sing when we praise*

Our nobody selves doing kind things,
unknown
Brings life to teary eyes, lightens shoulders
I will grin at clouds and paint its wonder
And write beautiful dreams that shout out
loud

This is my resistance, reverence and renewal

I am Sumaiyah Mohamed, Peer Support Specialist at Club HEAL. I was 19 when mental health mountains interrupted my adventures as a successful scholar of a student and budding bright-eyed adult. I developed schizophrenia and depression in my first semester. Being the type-A must-do-my-best student that I had always been, I put an intense amount of pressure on myself to produce excellent essays for a particular module to the point where over the course of that semester, I lost sleep, lost interest in anything that made me happy and I was always preoccupied with the thought that my essays were never ever good enough. It was a difficult time. In developing psychosis, I remember not feeling like I had to eat or go to the washroom, and I had the most horrible thoughts; I thought I was Satan and a murderer. I was confused.

When I think of how it all started, I cringe in grateful embarrassment. Trauma was not my childhood experience. I had a blessed time growing up with a village that enveloped my life with love and laughter – siblings that I admired and adored, sleepovers with my soulmate cousins, prayers and gatherings of remembrance, Barbie dolls, books, *teh susu* and *goreng pisang*, cycling in parks on weekends, and best of all, loving parents. I truly cherish my childhood.

The unconditional love of my family is among the factors that aided me in my recovery. Love to me is the most important of the values that Club HEAL stands for, *i.e.* hope, empowerment, acceptance, and love. H.E.A.L is also my formula to overcome my mental health challenges.

Love: indebted to infinity to my parents and support system

My parents lovingly but forcefully brought me to the hospital where I slowly recovered thanks to the light of God, and all the love from my support system, of course with various treatments, such as medication and electroconvulsive therapy. Though painful, I appreciate this experience. It turned my life around, and I truly feel it has made me a better person for it – now, I am very grateful for my parents, who loved me even when I was tremendously un-loveable, at my worst. My mother had taken my phone to call all my good friends to visit me, also all my aunts, uncles and cousins, even my school teachers, and neighbours, all of them who tenderly helped me to remember who I really was, enabling me to recover more heartily.

> *"Recovery is remembering who you are and using your strengths to become all you are meant to be."*

Acceptance: in recovery, ever vigilant

The shadow of depression does not disappear. Rather irritatingly, it shows up, quite like cockroaches at night in the kitchen. Despite a decade after diagnosis, I am still in recovery. I must remain vigilant - keep to my medication routine, watch out for warning signs, and importantly, practise self-care strategies that I keep in my wellness toolbox. I accept that depression is real for me and take up the challenge to take active steps to overcome it.

My psychiatrist, the energetic and motivational Dr Joseph Leong, inspired by Patricia Deegan, a psychologist, and an advocate of the mental health recovery movement, emphasised the importance of personal medicine. To me, while taking my 'pill medicine' received from the hospital is important, equally so is personal medicine which include non-pharmaceutical activities and strategies that decrease symptoms and increase personal wellness. For example, I really take to daily journaling because I feel it helps me understand why I had felt low that day or helps me release the negative thoughts occupying my mind. While journaling, I infuse positive energy within me as I write prayers and remember goodness. I also exercise, and I enjoy brisk walking. It makes me remember the different people I am grateful for in my life as I listen to soothing, positive music.

Hope: daily practice of writing, and of gratitude

I do two types of journaling each morning - the first being 'Morning Pages', a practice first espoused by Julia Cameron, an American artist. 'Morning Pages' is three pages of stream-of-consciousness writing, best done first thing in the morning before your day begins, where you pour out anything and everything that is in your mind and heart. For me, it allows me to express a lot of my negative thoughts freely, and then I feel lighter after. It is like a space where I can be as neurotic and worry as much as I need to, without judgment of myself. This writing is for my eyes only. The entries are sometimes similar - about my mood, about perhaps over-sleeping, about worries I have about work, about being a mother. It is a place where I can dump my every day, persistent worries. Although I write with no expectations, I am able to notice patterns and therefore take action to help myself towards wellness. For example, I notice if I wake up late, it ruins my mood. After a few days of waking up later than I intended to then cues me to take out my phone and set multiple alarms for the next day, to set me up for wellness.

Then I transition my writing into gratitude journaling where I list five things, I feel blessed about that day. It usually is an uplifting experience and I believe it trains my mind to remember the positive, to know I am loved, to cherish precious moments, to see wonder and joy in the everyday. Sometimes my gratitude journaling is also repetitive, favourites on the list being family members, coffee, writing itself, my current hobby (sewing) but I never feel bored writing them. I try to be as specific as I can with each item on the list - how they make me feel, what exactly I am grateful about for that thing/person.

This writing practice gives me hope each day. My worries are acknowledged and the beautiful things in my life are emphasised. And thus:

> ***I am grateful for***
> *My splintered heart*
> *The times my forehead finds itself on the floor*
> *Breezes of serenity, qasidas from my childhood*
> *Puzzles of prayers forgotten, Rumi poems found*
> *Stitched together making sense, finally*
> *The rhythm of spirits uplifted, xylophones, music*
> *Solace, my daughter's sheep soft-toy*
> *Did I already mention my daughter?*
> *My husband who lets me be real*
> *My mother and her mutton soup*
> *Faith, grace, and love, so much love*

Empowerment: purpose in peer support

Becoming a Peer Support Specialist, that is, a certified professional who has the lived experience of recovery from mental health challenges and uses her powerful story to empathise and empower another person in recovery, was one of the best things that has happened to me. The certification course was taught by a beautiful trainer from America, the wonderful, lovable, and affirming Chris Martin. He taught us that peer support was a calling, a sacred responsibility, and each interaction with a person we are journeying with was something to be deeply intentional about. He showed me that really listening with a present heart, showing our understanding through our listening, relating with empathy, and affirming strengths of each other is so powerfully transformative and healing. The idea of my job being part of a higher purpose gave me the motivation to keep working daily in my work of supporting fellow people in recovery, through dark days and through times when I felt I was not making any impact.

It means everything to me to know that there is a place for me, and that my experiences can teach someone in some way, even if I am reminding only myself, and that it can guide and reassure that brighter days exist, that power resides deep and well within us. Healing and recovery may seem difficult, but it can be as simple as an appreciation for the everyday and seemingly small things in life.

Medicine
Honey
Glass of water
Oatmeal
Coffee
Family to live for
Work waiting for me
Prayer - do not forget it is air
Breaths and quiet
Book in my bag

Also, my pen and journal
Poetry
Friends
Enthusiasm and zest!
Endurance
Giggles with my daughter
Gasps, of wonder
Journeys - be a traveller
Never stop movement

13

FROM DARKNESS TO LIGHT – FROM ADDICT TO REHABILITATOR

I am Faizal Abdul Rahim, 51, a Programme Executive at Club HEAL, and this is the story of my healing from drug addiction and depression. Indeed, I have come a long way and I would like to share my journey since my troubled youth to the present.

Good childhood memories

My childhood was wonderful. My parents were teachers and we would go for holidays every end of the year during the school vacations. During primary school, I excelled in track and field and other sports. The happiest moment in my life was when we from Monk's Hill Secondary School defeated Raffles Institution in the 1983 National

Hockey Finals. I was the left-wing striker. My coach called me "Lethal Weapon".

Troubled teen

Unfortunately, I was sent to the Reformative Training Centre (RTC) towards the end of my secondary school for attempted robbery. I had gotten into bad company and had become very rebellious towards my mother, whom I perceived as an authoritarian. I was supposed to be incarcerated for 24–36 months but was given a reprieve when, having studied as a private candidate for the 'O' level examination at the RTC, my results qualified me for junior college. However, I could not break my bad habits. I was from RTC, where guys fought almost all the time. Life outside the RTC was no different for me, I was in a gang and continued fighting. Soon, I dropped out of school.

Job-hopper

Since I could not find a good job without relevant skills or qualifications, I skipped from job to job. I worked as a salesman, security guard, delivery assistant, in factory production lines, *etc.*

I felt regretful. I had lost touch with most of my friends from school. I had disappointed my parents by not continuing my studies. There was also the feeling of worthlessness, partly because the friends still had worked at jobs Singaporeans generally shunned.

My parents did not give up on me. They brought me for a visit to the holy city of Mecca in the hope of inspiring me to change. Yes, it was a terrific experience. Many have found a pilgrimage to be a turning point in their lives but not for me; it did not stop my drug addiction, which started in 1989 when I first took marijuana.

Heroin addiction

When heroin flowed into Singapore, I tried it out of curiosity, but alas I was hooked on it and was caught several times. The laws were harsh in the early days and drug addicts were treated like hardened criminals. The Drug Rehabilitation Centres (DRCs) used regimental treatment and there was no proper counselling available to help us. I feel the prison's rehab routine was not suitable for making addicts into better human beings. Instead, I fell into depression.

Depression and drugs

Depression saw me being admitted into the hospitals for more than ten times in ten years. I was given Electro Convulsive Therapy (ECT) many times and I was on heavy medication. I became dysfunctional. Whenever I was out of hospital, heroin and psychotropic drugs became my daily consumption and I could not stay on any job for long.

In between these relapses, my parents sent me to Australia to pursue a diploma in the fine arts. They thought a regional change might help me. I remember I only attended classes two or three times only, before I found company among drug addicts again. Australia at that time was heaven for heroin addicts. I shot the drug intravenously every day. My father witnessed my deterioration in Australia, so he brought me home to Singapore. I was already 27 years old by then.

Family support

My parents still did not give up on me. They spent thousands of dollars trying to get me treated. I never enjoyed my 20s because I was in and out of prison and DRCs for most of the period. My last admission into the DRC was in 2012. That was the 6th time I was sent to the DRC.

Reading to recovery

This time in the DRC, I decided to resume a long-forgotten hobby, reading, which my mother had encouraged when was a child. In the DRC, I accessed the library frequently and searched for self-help books. Maybe age played a part, but I think those readings had opened a region in my mind that was closed; the region of realization. After being discharged, I decided to change my life.

A new life

I enrolled as a member in a gym in Singapore. I trained hard, ate well and slept well. I developed well-toned muscles and began to look much better.

I also did volunteer work at a well-known outpatient day care centre for people who were recovering from illness. I facilitated sing-along sessions, which were well-received. Even those who were detached from the group would eventually join in. Many requested songs from me, and I would take time to learn the songs I did not know to make them happy.

Counselling and hypnotherapy

In my early 40s, I decided to pursue a Specialist Diploma in Counselling Psychology. I graduated with high distinction. After that, I took an advanced hypnotherapy course and graduated as a master hypnotist and a certified consulting hypnotist under the National Guild of Hypnotists, Inc, and am now able to use hypnotherapy to treat people.

I did not stop there. With my Specialist Diploma in Counselling Psychology, I was accepted to do a postgraduate program with the Executive Counselling and Training Academy (ECTA), Singapore. I also obtained a Graduate Diploma of Social Science in Professional Counselling, a postgraduate degree accredited by Swinburne University of Technology, Melbourne, Australia.

Music therapy

Eventually, I was employed as a counsellor with Club HEAL. My job was wonderful, helping those with mental health challenges. I facilitated "Music Therapy" and held the positions of counsellor and music instructor. As a music instructor doing expressive therapy, I would get the clients to sing along and, slowly but surely, those who were detached from others began to mix around, started singing together and became cheerful again. I also structured a choir program where the clients performed on stage during festive celebrations. We performed twice in the presence of the President of Singapore, Madam Halimah Yacob. I was happy to see peers regain their self-esteem and confidence through their participation in the weekly Music Therapy.

Lost in love

Then, I suffered a relapse. The reason was my divorce. I remarried a woman I had loved 27 years earlier and hoped we could settle into a long loving relationship, but the marriage lasted only a year. The divorce blunted my focus, and prevented me from obtaining the Master of Counselling that I was pursuing. I also could not continue with my job as a counsellor at Club HEAL. I was admitted into hospital again for depression. I had never felt that kind of sadness in my life.

God, The Healer

Now I am healed, although it was exceedingly difficult to get up again after a rock bottom fall. I had to develop a complete trust in the goodness of God. I believed God would heal me and I was, but the healing process was a painful one. Alhamdulillah, Club HEAL offered me a job again, as Programme Executive.

I hope this journey to recovery will inspire others who are travelling on a similar path and need to get their lives back on track. Addictions and depression are hard to overcome, but with the tenacity to move forward, life can and will change for the better. Don't give up. Trust God. He can rebuild your life, no matter how you are right now.

14

MASSIVE STROKE, MASSIVE TRANSFORMATION

The 10-year journey of caring for her father who had two strokes inspired Siti Hazirah Bte Mohamad, 32, to do research in palliative care, a form of care that aims to improve the quality of life of patients with life-limiting illnesses, and their caregivers. His strokes, the first when she was only 22, transformed her life and in turn helps her in attempting to transform the lives of others.

Hazirah's father, Mohamad Bin Ab Rahman, 59, a senior technician, had a severe stroke in 2010. The impact was great – the doctors gave him a 50/50 chance of survival pre-surgery as the blood clot in his brain had burst. A surgical procedure was performed to remove a section of his skull to relieve the pressure and swelling in his brain. The section was restored six months later.

Said Hazirah, a research associate, "Thankfully, he survived the surgery – but it took a massive toll on him. He lost almost all his powers of speech, memory, reasoning and thinking. He was also fully paralysed on the right side of his body and remains so till this day."

A life transformed

Hazirah was having summer school at a university in Mexico when she received news that her father was fighting for his life. "When I finally reached the ICU (Intensive Care Unit) and saw my Dad, the deep sense of grief was suddenly replaced with clarity – I knew that things had changed irrevocably, and that there was no turning back. I allowed myself to cry for another 30 minutes, then wiped my tears and rolled up my sleeves. It was time to get to work, as the eldest child."

A multitude of factors, including untreated hyperthyroidism, heavy smoking and high cholesterol had contributed to Mohamad's stroke. At the beginning of his recovery journey, mentally, he was disoriented and confused and was most likely suffering from post-stroke depression. This depressive episode meant that he initially did not want to take part in rehabilitation and was overly aggressive and temperamental. "There was also a period of time in which we noticed significant mood changes and hallucinations – we were referred to a neurologist who was also a psychiatrist." The latter suggested antidepressants but Hazirah's family chose non-pharmaceutical ways to alleviate his mood swings.

As for her family, his illness shook them to the core. "Overnight, my mother, who had been a housewife for more than 20 years, became the new head of the family. She had to make decisions that she was not used to making, in an incredibly stressful and emotionally difficult time. I had been overseas for more than a year and, at that point, had to combat jet lag, shock and grief, and make a hundred big and small decisions with regards to my father's care, our family's finances, and also our wellbeing. Saying that we were thrown into the deep end was an understatement."

A student, a caregiver

Hazirah had to assume many responsibilities and juggle caregiving with studying. Despite objections from some friends and family members, she pursued her dream of getting a Master's degree instead of working to support the family immediately. She said, "I was determined not to be a martyr but instead made decisions that would both support my interests *and* my family's needs. Thankfully, my mother eventually came round to the idea and supported my aspirations." Hazirah added that she did not want to resent her father for the choice she could have otherwise made and at the same time, she was determined not to compromise on his care.

Perseverance pays

Caring for her father has been a very fulfilling learning journey. Said Hazirah, "This decade long caregiving journey has taught me a lot about the value of perseverance – long after many had given up, my father managed to do things that might seemed unfathomable – from learning to walk again, to communicating non-verbally but effectively with us, and also to eating again, after close to ten years of tube-feeding."

"This is nothing short of remarkable – just when I thought my father had reached the end of his recovery threshold (his doctors and the literature told us that the biggest recovery would usually happen in the first year post-stroke, and the condition that he's in after a year would probably be the one that he would remain in for the rest of his life), my father continued to surprise us. He learnt to walk again about three years post-stroke and continued to make significant cognitive gains up to ten years post-stroke. His strength in beating the odds inspired me to want to push harder to ensure that he received the care he deserved."

A second setback

Unfortunately, Mohamad was struck with a second stroke in 2019. This time, it was on the right side of his brain, which meant that the other side of his body was also affected, which complicated walking for him. "However, an unexpected thing happened – my father learnt to eat again, after ten years! This was generally a very rare occurrence, and it brought tears to my eyes to see him eat his first few mouthfuls. He also learnt how to walk a second time, beating the odds," shared Hazirah.

However, a few weeks after he was brought home from the community hospital, where he was undergoing rehabilitation, Mohamad started to suffer a series of falls and appeared to be getting weaker."

Surprises in store

However, she remained hopeful for improvements in his health. "Thanks to the valuable lessons on patience and gratitude that I had obtained from the first episode, I knew that I had to take things slow, and to always keep the faith, as the outcomes might surprise me immensely, even beyond the limits of my comprehension," she said confidently.

Gratitude thus played a big part in her own acceptance of her father's condition. "While I am devastated that my father has suffered two strokes, I reminded myself to always be grateful that we had been given the chance to have him around. Sometimes my father does the smallest of gestures that reminds us of the person that he was – and that brings back such vivid memories of his character. I am glad to know that some things never change."

She added, "We always remind him that he has been really blessed to have another chance at life. We encourage him to exercise autonomy too, even by non-verbal means such as in choosing TV programmes or food. These might seem small, but to me they are significant as it demonstrates that he still has free will and self-determination despite having suffered severe limitations."

Recovery for any patient – and healing for their family – is never easy. Hazirah mused, "Oftentimes, people see the end result, which is after all the hard work and all the blood, sweat and tears have been expended. However, the journey and process are as important as the destination: invest time and energy in healing, and it would provide you with a foundation to buttress you against further storms ahead."

Strong support system

Indeed, she braved storms with a strong support system. "My mother has nerves of steel and the constitution of iron. Every time I felt that I had reached the end of the rope, she reminded me that there was still more to gain, if only we practice acceptance and patience."

Hazirah also relied on a group of close friends who became her pillar of strength. Most of them have been with her for many years and have witnessed her family's journey. She also had friends who were healthcare providers and she was able to share her experiences in caregiving with them when they faced challenges. "In fact, I managed to give suggestions for their problems based on adaptations that I had developed for my father," she said.

Caregiving and burnout

Her mother, her siblings and Hazirah sometimes disagree on what is the best care for Mohamad, but they know that the conflicts come from a place of love, with her father's best interests at heart. "This is an important point to remember, especially in times of great stress, exhaustion and tension. The journey of caregiving for my father would not have been possible without their support. Caregiving, especially for a person with severe cognitive impairment, is hard and burnout is an ever-present reality. It's important to look out for each other's wellbeing and think of caregiving as a relay race or tag team, in which one can pass the baton to the next person and take turns to assume responsibilities."

Path to a career in palliative care

The path to her present job was not only inspired by her father but by her grandmother whose health started deteriorating three years after her dad fell ill. "As her condition worsened and her care needs became more complex, I found that because of my prior experience with my father's care, it was easy for me to transfer these skills to support my aunts and uncles in caring for her. I was very grateful that the knowledge which I had obtained painstakingly over the years was being put to good use," said Hazirah.

While in the hospital, her grandmother was eventually transferred to a palliative care team. That was her first exposure to this branch of medicine. "This, despite the fact that between my father and grandmother at that point, I must have seen more than ten different specialists!" she said.

She felt that palliative care combined the biomedical aspect of medicine with its social and human core beautifully. Said Hazirah, "This is why I chose it as my vocation; I felt that the work that I do aligns with my values and allows me to put my beliefs into practice."

Empathy and contributing to society

Hazirah has sat in panels and taken part in research conducted by organisations like AWARE (Association of Women for Action and Research) to share her caregiving experience and its challenges. "I always urged others to learn from my mistakes so that they do not have to go through the whole rigmarole all over again."

"My father's illness taught me to empathise with the people whom I did research with – when I told them that I understood the challenges they faced while caregiving, I was not merely paying lip service, I too experienced the same situation at home! We exchanged insights and tips on caregiving," said Hazirah.

The need for national initiatives

Caregivers are often told to just endure their hardships, and that the rewards would come later. "While this could be useful, it could also come across as quite dismissive – it invalidates the struggles that many caregivers go through and dismisses the immense challenges that we face in caring for a loved one. I think it's time for a national reckoning on how tough caregiving is, both for the young and old, and question the notion of care spaces – who gets to inhabit them, and who provides them," she asserted.

"I hope to work towards getting more support for caregivers from the national and societal aspects to ensure that caregiving responsibilities are more evenly distributed. Empowerment is crucial – the more caregivers feel that they have a stake in the care landscape in Singapore, the better the solutions developed to cater to their needs will be."

15

TAKING CHARGE THROUGH SELF-AWARENESS

I am Shari Almashoor, 61, and I am a hypnotherapist/counsellor. I started volunteering with Club HEAL from Day One, when it was first set up in 2012. I facilitate classes on Awareness. Due to my frequent travels I can only commit to volunteering whenever I am in Singapore.

A.F.A.L

My classes at Club HEAL is all about awareness, forgiveness, acceptance and letting it go with love. Hence, I came up with the application of A.F.A.L., which is healing from within.

My focus is on helping peers understand that they can take charge of their own thought process and overcome their suffering naturally with simple daily practices which I share in my sessions. When I see even one person making a breakthrough it just gives me joy and I know life is simply worth living.

Becoming whole

To me, healing is a more therapeutic way of becoming whole and recovery is to reinstate what is lost or taken physically or emotionally. Spiritual healing is more powerful as it goes to the root cause, which requires faith and devotion in oneself.

As a hypnotherapist, I usually go with my intuition on what application to help with my clients. I would like to share one case where I had an urgent call from a client. She said she needed to see me in her office during lunch time, as she was always busy. So, I had to work with the time constraint.

She had felt a lump under her left breast, and it was giving her some discomfort. She had made a doctor's appointment the following week but at that moment, she was full of anxiety and worry, anticipating the worst. Firstly, I calmed her down with basic hypnosis. Then she was able to share in more detail what was causing her anxiety and worry. After about 15 minutes of sharing I knew that standard procedure hypnosis was not the right treatment, so I got her to do Effective Freedom Technique or Tapping (EFT). We went about four rounds of EFT with simple deep breathing and at the end of the session she screamed with excitement which took me by surprise as I thought she was in pain. The truth was, she was excited that the pain was gone although the lump was still there. What a relief! I insisted that she kept her doctor's appointment. A few days after her doctor's visit she called to let me know how grateful she was and that she could manage her worry and anxiety as it arose.

Awareness

At my first session of volunteer work at Club HEAL @ Bukit Batok East I had no idea how small or large a group I would be working with, so I had to be prepared for all eventualities. Using my intuition, I decided to go with the flow of energy of the participants so that they could enjoy a truly interactive session.

When someone asked me then what my session was called, I joked, "*Nothing* Coming". I knew I did not want to name it mindfulness as I do not like the idea of the mind being full, which *create*s problems. Now I call the session AWARENESS, for it seems most apt.

Only through being aware of your situation can you start to get help and make the necessary steps and changes for yourself.

My sessions are all about being open and honest to yourself, accepting your situation and finding solutions – including healthy eating, basic body movements and laughter – all of which are frequently underrated, despite having a positive effect on mental and overall health. I also incorporate repetition of breathing exercises; practising being grateful, humble, and forgiving with positive affirmations; and living in the Now.

We are the most sophisticated and comfortable creatures on earth, and I enjoy reminding the peers about this constantly, so they do not take anything for granted.

Memory and Imagination

The two most fundamental roots of human sufferings are (a) vivid memories (be it negative or positive, as our subconscious mind cannot differentiate between the two); and (b) our capacity to imagine. Our whole being is about accumulation of outside information. An excessive reliance on memory (past experience) and imagination (your own creation of a possible future or an exaggerated past) can easily lead to mental confusion. Therefore, it can become incredibly challenging for some to manage on their own without outside assistance.

Club HEAL centres offer many ways of assisting participants to overcome such challenges through counselling, rehab sessions and support groups. These sessions give them an opportunity to express themselves without being judged or labelled.

Faith in God

Throughout my volunteer services with Club HEAL, I find great satisfaction when some participants make positive progress to be back in the society or to be an integral part of Club HEAL. It is all about giving back what we have received. The Cycle of Life is essentially about giving out good so that good returns to you. Having faith in the power of a Merciful and Powerful God makes that journey a reality.

Rewards

It is so rewarding whenever I receive a text message or a note to say how much the peers appreciate my classes and are taking small positive steps to be in control of their journey, applying what they have learnt. It shows that they have understood the message I want to share: that changes start with them and it is ultimately about choices, no matter what the situation they are in.

Before I end, let me share one of my many daily affirmations: *"Today is the day of my amazing good fortune."* Try it regularly, and see your own amazing good fortune open up before you, with God's permission!

16

UNDYING SPIRIT TO HELP OTHERS RECOVER

Counsellor at Club HEAL, Nurleen bte Mohamad feels blessed to have witnessed the recovery of many of her clients. "To me recovery is not about eliminating or removing the diagnosis totally, but it is about having an unfailing spirit to continue their recovery journey despite the struggles. Many of them become a source of inspiration to us counsellors as well."

Nurleen, who is in her thirties, has worked for four years in Club HEAL, after switching from the logistics industry to pursue her true passion. Her interest in counselling began when she was a volunteer at a Family Service Centre. She now holds a degree in counselling.

There is a difference between healing and recovery for Nurleen. "Recovery is the ongoing drive to continue to grow and flourish despite the odds. Healing on the other hand means no longer being affected by former 'wounds'," she notes.

Multiple factors cause mental illnesses

Nurleen explained that different factors cause one to develop mental health conditions. They include, among others, biological factors, family history, hormonal changes, and life experiences such as losses or trauma. Prolonged unmanaged stress is one such factor. "We are exposed to stress daily, such as work stress, relationship stress, school stress, family situations. With good social support from family, friends or society, some of us are able to manage this stress. Some, however – due to their circumstances – may not have the privilege of accessing such support. Unyielding stress over an extended period can lead to mental health conditions in *anyone*," she stresses.

Traits that aid in recovery

A client's personality plays an important part in the recovery process. "In my experience, people of various personalities can recover. Nevertheless, the attribute of humility plays an important role. Humility allows one to be receptive to learning new skills and understanding that no one is superior to another. In fact, acquiring humility will inevitably garner respect from others."

We are our own worst critic

An attitude of patience is also a must in the recovery journey. "We are often our own worst critic. Exercising patience towards oneself is about tolerating distress and understanding that recovery does not usually happen smoothly nor in a linear manner. Regressions are expected to happen. There will be days when it just feels like we are back at where we started off. However, by exercising patience and being nurturing towards oneself, clients learn to motivate themselves instead of being enmeshed in self-blame and self-loathing."

Struggles with demons of the past

Coming to terms with a difficult past or experiences is often a daunting task for many of us. "I have seen the struggles that one has to endure just to come to terms with them. Processing the difficult past and/or changing the perspective of life experiences help some clients. Instead of remaining a victim of the past, they learn to view these experiences differently, for example, by seeing lessons in them instead."

Leading by example

Nurleen tries to help her clients understand the importance of patience and gratitude by exemplifying these traits. "I must say I still struggle with this at times. I definitely believe if we are able to demonstrate these qualities in our interactions with clients and others, it will influence them because they will feel the effect."

Different types of interventions

Different clients require different interventions, depending on the individual's (a) level of awareness or insight; (b) commitment to change and improvement; and (c) cognitive competency due to severity of the illness. Interventions are tailored based on the collaborative understanding between clients and counsellors. Early interventions for those who have been formally diagnosed is very helpful in assisting them to recover. "Interventions differ, depending on the uniqueness of the presenting issue, the support required, the client's goals, *etc.*" said Nurleen.

There are different counselling approaches, depending on the client's suitability and the counsellor's training background. Said Nurleen, "Significant improvements can be seen in some clients when they are provided with an avenue to release strong emotions (catharsis effect) as it provides them with a sense of relief. Others require more frequent and intense interventions (*e.g.*, utilising counselling approaches and frameworks). In essence, it is about collaborative work between the client and counsellor, where together we reflect upon actions and their significance, the counselling process and ways to meet the counselling goals."

Family matters

Family involvement in a client's recovery is important. Family who are able to provide their loved ones emotional support and regularly meet up with counsellors improve the chances of the clients' recovery. Nurleen advises, "Openly discuss with counsellors how, as a family, you can help your loved ones. Be open to the possible changes required, such as in communication."

Relating one case where the caregiver made a great impact on her child's recovery, Nurleen said, "I remember meeting up with a caregiver whose child was diagnosed with psychosis. The caregiver felt that the family situation caused her daughter's mental condition. She could have gone into a self-blaming state, but, she took the initiative to learn new skills to help her daughter. She regularly attended caregivers' support group, improved on her communication with her daughter and acknowledged the small progress made by her daughter, thereby exercising gratitude openly. We saw the improvements, gradually. My client is now more receptive to medication and can perform her own activities of daily living (ADL). The caregiver's undying love and patience, not only towards her daughter, *but also towards herself*, helped my client in her recovery journey."

Nurleen emphasises that positive changes do not happen overnight. "It takes patience, unceasing hope and consistent gratitude, and *magnifying seemingly insignificant* improvements."

Role of rehabilitation

Rehabilitation activities complement counselling sessions. For example, clients who are diagnosed with social anxiety will benefit from joining the rehabilitation activities, where they learn how to socialise in a safe environment (the rehabilitative centre). Through rehabilitation, one gets to explore their potential and capability in a nurturing setting. This will help to increase their confidence and self-esteem, which is beneficial for their mental wellbeing.

My journey with Club HEAL

Club HEAL runs supports groups (including the Youth Support Group and the Caregiver Support Group) and empowerment programmes (*e.g.*, Our Healing Voice). Support groups provide clients and caregivers with emotional and psychological support and allow them to meet others with similar experiences or of the same age group. Empowerment programmes provide clients with a platform to further acquire coping strategies skills and nurture them to be Mental Health Advocates to inspire others.

For Nurleen, it has been a rewarding four years at Club HEAL. She continues to grow and be inspired by her work. "Listening to clients and caregivers sharing has made me reflect upon my own life: how I handle situations, how my own actions can impact another person's life. It has made me more mindful of my actions and allowed me to reflect upon my intentions."

"Prior to this career change, it was easy to judge others for their unacceptable behaviour. However, through my studies and interactions with the people I counsel, I understand that there is often a story behind a person's actions and behavioural changes," says this introvert, who likes to chill with a book in a café or take strolls in the park on weekends.

Not a mental advocate but an ally

For Nurleen, a mental health advocate is someone who tirelessly work in educating the public about mental health in hope to eradicate stigma and promote mental health management. They are inspiring individuals, not only in the work that they have done or doing, but also in their own personal life as well.

"I do not consider myself as a mental health advocate but more of an ally who supports those who undergo mental health difficulties. Some of my friends and family have voiced their concern for my psychological and physical 'safety' when I first embarked on my career as a mental health counsellor – as if mental illness is contagious!" she noted with a laugh.

"However, after seeing that I am still in this line after four years, their concerns have gradually subsided. I feel that has reduced the stigma surrounding mental health conditions, at least for the people around me. Being able to share the minimal knowledge and experience about mental health has been a privilege."

17

PATIENCE AND GRATITUDE, THE ISLAMIC WAY

Sabr

Sabr is the Arabic word for patience. *Sabr* comes from a root word meaning "to refrain and stop." So, patience is a virtue which helps us to refrain from doing that which is not good. "Being patient is a challenge for many of us. We are encouraged to do so with the rewards of attaining Heaven and Allah's companionship," says Ustazah Shameem Sultanah binte Abdul Gafoor, 36, a motivational Islamic speaker.

"We all have two forces inside of us. One is the 'driving force' which pushes us forward to act, and the other is a 'restraining force' which holds us back," explains Ustazah Shameem, 36. "Patience utilises the driving force to push ourselves towards good deeds, and the restraining force to prevent ourselves from doing bad deeds."

Islam enjoins patience in the face of tests.

Allah says in the Quran:

> "And We will surely test you with something of fear and hunger and a loss of wealth and lives and fruits – but give good tidings to the patient, who, when disaster strikes them, say, 'Indeed we belong to Allah, and indeed to Him we will return.'" [al-Baqarah: 115 & 156]

Syukr

Syukr is the Arabic word for gratitude, namely, being thankful to Allah for all His blessings. There are three levels of gratitude or thankfulness. The first level is the appreciation we feel in our hearts. Then, we fortify that thankfulness through our speech. And the third level is when we prove by our deeds that we are truly thankful to God.

Ustazah Shameem explains, "Gratitude is the *choice* to focus on the positive aspects of life. It is a reminder that every time we feel like complaining, we should count our blessings instead. And when we do that, we will realise that there are simply too many to count."

Allah Himself says:

> "And if you should count the favours of Allah, you could not enumerate them. Indeed, Allah is Forgiving and Merciful." [an-Nahl: 18]

Indeed, God is with those who are grateful.

> *"And [remember] when your Lord proclaimed, 'If you are grateful, I will surely increase you [in favour]'"* [Ibrahim: 7]

And He says:

> *"So, remember Me; I will remember you. And be grateful to Me and do not deny Me."* [al-Baqarah: 152]

Healing versus recovery

What is the difference between recovery and healing? Ustazah Shameem sees it this way. "If you're trying to restore yourself to the person you were before you got hurt, you're trying to recover. If you are ready to shed your old self and become someone entirely new, you are ready to heal. Healing is choosing what nourishes you and restoring relationships instead of walking away from problems. Healing is finding unprecedented worth and power. Healing is stepping into what you have never done before. Healing is a rebirth."

Ustazah Shameem loves this quote from Brianna West:

> *"Recovering is important, but it isn't permanent. Healing is essential because it lasts forever."*

Purposeful wounds and scars

Illness and challenging life experiences will definitely leave scars and wounds that are yet to heal. As Muslims, we believe that these wounds serve a purpose. Allah has not created anything in vain, not even illness. There is a purpose to these struggles. Allah says:

> "And We did not create the heaven and the earth and that between them aimlessly."
> [*Swad*: 27]

"Compare these struggles to the purification of gold. The gold needs to be heated up in an extreme temperature so that the impurities can be easily separated from the pure gold. Our hearts are similar. Without these afflictions and calamities, we will be too comfortable and will not be pushed to our knees to surrender to Allah and rely on Him completely – which is how we become closer to Him" says Ustazah Shameem.

Even bad things happen only with His permission

Allah created everything, even those who do evil in this world. It is He who gives us illness, be it physical or mental. And He is the One who cures.

> "And when I am ill, it is He who cures me."
> [*Asyu'ara:* 80]

Constriction and expansion

One of the words that is used in the Quran to signify psychological stress is *daqat* which means to become "narrow, confined, constricted and tight".

Ustazah Shameem says, "So, when our chest and mind are constricted, we need to work on expanding them. And for muscles to expand, they need to be relaxed. As Muslims, we believe that the remembrance of Allah relaxes our mind and soul." Allah says in the Quran:

> *"Those who have believed and whose hearts are reassured by the remembrance of Allah … indeed, by the remembrance of Allah, hearts are assured."* [*ar-Ra'd*: 28]

So, internalising the meaning of the Quran is important. Remembering that Allah is always with us and that Allah loves us helps in low times.

> *"So, remember Me; I will remember you. And be grateful to Me and do not deny Me."* [*al-Baqarah*: 152]

Why mental illness is different

Since physical illnesses are external, people find it easier to comprehend them, unlike mental illnesses, which are internal and hard to perceive … especially when a person exhibits no physical disability.

"Compare this to a computer. A cracked screen may be easy to repair compared to a fault with the motherboard. Mental illness affects the brain and is harder to see and understand. Often, we give up without putting in real effort at seeking a suitable cure," says Ustazah Shameen.

But as Muslims, we are taught to believe that there is a solution to every problem, challenge, and illness.

Allah says in the Quran:

> *"And whoever is conscious of Allah, He will make for him a way out. And will provide for him from places he does not expect. And whoever relies on Allah, then He is sufficient for him. Indeed, Allah will accomplish His purpose. Allah has already set for everything a [decreed] extent."* [al-Talaq: 2-3]

Allah is Most Loving

"I am not an expert in mental health from the medical perspective. So, when people approach me on mental health issues, I focus on just one thing – letting them know how much Allah loves them and that they need to be closer to Him. And there is no better way to really let this sink in than manifesting patience and gratitude in our lives. It is like a fuel in this life journey. Also, on this journey, we must stop when the lights are red and adhere to all the traffic rules patiently to reach our destination; we need that kind of patience when we are stopped by life challenges," says Ustazah Shameem.

Life is not a competition

"We must focus on our lane and stop comparing ourselves to others. Then only can gratitude be manifested. This life is not a competition. Our life challenges are tailored by Allah and He has promised us that He will never burden us beyond our capacity," adds Ustazah Shameem.

Acceptance in the face of trials

Sharing a story, Ustazah Shameem says, "I know of a lady whose husband jumped to his death with her one-year-old daughter whom she had given birth to after ten years of marriage. She witnessed them exhaling their last breath but she was not crying. I then asked her, what made her so strong? And she told me these beautiful words: 'Didn't Allah promised that He will not burden us beyond our capacity?'

Indeed, the Quran says:

> *"Allah does not charge a soul except [with that within] its capacity."* [al-Baqarah: 286]

Reflects Ustazah Shameem, "Many of us recite these verses of the Qur'an regularly, but the real difference is that she believed in Him. She believed in

His words, in His promise. And just by internalising that, she was able to heal and become stronger. And that is to me, an example of patience and gratitude healing a mental and emotional pain."

Ustazah Shameem also reminds us not to underestimate the power of *du'a*:

> *O you who have believed, seek help through patience and prayer. Indeed, Allah is with the patient.* [Al-Baqarah: 153]

Coping through religion

Religion plays an important coping mechanism in times of stress. Religion helps explain concepts such as evil, suffering, guilt and forgiveness. Spirituality provides a source of comfort and helps one heal from a traumatic experience; offering hope and optimism and gives meaning and purpose to the event. It also makes us realise our limits as humans and leads us to surrender to the One God who has no limits to His Power, Knowledge and Wisdom.

Researchers have found that collaborative religious coping has the most benefit for the individual's physical and mental health. This means that the person relies upon God while at the same time attempting to do his or her part to change or cope with the situation. This is the Islamic way.

Deferring and self-directing have negative consequences

Other methods such as deferring (when the individual takes a passive role in the coping efforts and waits for God to control the situation) and self-directing (seeking control through individual initiative instead of help from God) have been found to aggravate the health problems.

Good in every bad

The Prophet Muhammad (pbuh) said:

> *"How amazing is the affair of the believer. Everything is good for him – and that is for no one but the believer. If good times comes his way, he is thankful and that is good for him, and if hardship comes his way, he is patient and that is good for him."* [*Muslim*]

Thus, everything that happens to us, even things that seem to be bad, are in fact good for us.

"You might not see the good when you are sad. You might not see it when you have just suffered a loss. That is what *Syaithan* (the Devil) wants you to focus on – he want you to conclude that Allah hates you; that Allah does not give you the favours He gives to others because He does not like you. *Syaithan* wants you to move away from God," warns Ustazah Shameem.

His everlasting love

"But Allah is *Ar-Rahman* (The Most Gracious) and *Ar-Raheem* (The Most Compassionate). Know that He loves us tremendously, beyond our imagination and cares for us all the time, not only this world but in the Hereafter. With patience in the face of life's trials and gratitude to Allah, there is a cure for every illness."

18

HEALING IS REAL

Healing takes time, notes Professor Chua Hong Choon, 55, psychiatrist and chief executive officer (CEO) of the Institute of Mental Health (IMH). This is because some of the contributing causes of a person's mental health problems could be deep rooted. "Recovery may take some time. We must give our patients time to heal. It is hard to tell them to be patient though, for they have probably been suffering for a long time."

Illness signature

Every patient has an illness signature – a unique pattern of his or her illness. For instance, A had a traumatic event in his life and he subsequently became frequently suicidal. B on the other hand, has bipolar disorder with frequent manic episodes. C might be afflicted with a mental condition more because of genetic factors. D may have depression because of childhood abuse. "Thus, the road to recovery differs for each patient who has different genetic backgrounds and different life experiences," said Prof Chua.

Being yourself

Acceptance certainly plays an important part in the recovery and healing process, which, to Prof Chua, are much the same thing. "Healing is achieved when you become the person you are meant to be. In other words, you are being yourself." A person may still be under treatment while he is healed from the emotional wounds of the past.

Different stigma

Looking at the Singapore society today, Prof Chua reckoned that there is still significant stigma against persons with mental illness. "But the stigma is different today. Twenty years ago, people believed that mental illness was due to demonic possession and the work of evil spirits, and that the mentally ill were violent and dangerous. Now, it is more common to believe that persons with mental health problems are less valuable to society; they are seen as being unreliable, so they are not to be given jobs or included in society."

An affable man with a smile for everybody, Prof Chua was initially a doctor in the emergency room but felt the call of psychiatry when he had family members and friends who experienced mental health issues. "I wanted to help people heal and regain their lives; I wanted to do this with kindness," he said.

Treat with kindness

Indeed, being kind and patient to people with mental health issues can make all the difference in the recovery process. When relapses happen, it is usually because of a stimulus or trigger which oftentimes, comes from the home. "The patients may face rejection, fear, depression, loss and need to regain control of their emotions," he said. This is where caregivers, family and friends need to show extra care and kindness.

Spirituality helps

Prof Chua said that spirituality or religion plays an important part in helping patients accept their condition. "It is like when you are drowning. The more you struggle, the more you sink. But if you relax, you will find yourself safe and afloat." Spirituality plays a big part in keeping patients calm at times of difficulty," he said.

In cases where there are frequent relapses, it is hard to determine the causes of them, but it could be due to the neurotransmitters which had been drastically changed because of trauma or life experiences. Sometimes, it is more in the genes, where family members have mental illnesses. Some of these conditions may have positive aspects to it, as people with bipolar disorder are thought to be highly creative.

Positive changes

Prof Chua is happy that things are looking up for those with mental health conditions in Singapore. "I am an optimistic person. There is increasing awareness of the importance of mental health, and mental wellbeing is being highlighted and promoted in the community," he observed.

On a personal note, his journey with his patients has not been a one-way street. "I gain a lot of knowledge and experience from my patients," said Prof Chua.

Prof Chua said counting one's blessings and keeping a positive outlook are important especially for patients as they struggle with big challenges. Being grateful and patient makes a lot of difference. "Between two patients who suffer the same condition, the one that shows these two traits recover faster as they help make the mood more stable. It is important for all of us to foster patience and gratitude as they help us cope with our daily lives."

19

I AM NOT BIPOLAR, I AM YOHANNA

I am not bipolar. I think I have come to this conclusion after my 22 years struggle with Bipolar Disorder Type 1. This means I am more prone to high moods than low moods. While I have an illness that causes me depression and mania, I am not the illness. You do not call a cancer patient, cancerous, so why should you call me bipolar? But I guess it is easier to say that rather than 'a person with bipolar disorder'. But all labels are foggy, ill-fitting, and can stigmatise or scar a person.

Just Yohanna

Thus, I prefer to be known as simply Yohanna, or Yoyo, a fun, pleasant, positive, and kind person (if I may say so myself, ha ha) who has lived experience of a mental illness of the bipolar variety. When I was manic, I went on wild, spending sprees, was sexually explicit and sang and danced in public. When I was depressed, I stayed in my bed most of the time and found it difficult to eat, bathe, do chores, and take care of my children. In between the highs and lows are periods of normal moods where I am moderate, rational and at my best. Since early last year, I have been in my normal phase. My symptoms have abated after my worst ever year in 2018 when I had three episodes of mania within seven months. I was hospitalised in the Mood Disorder Unit (MDU) of the Institute of Mental Health (IMH). I reckoned I was having too much fun and stress at work and in my personal life while having long-term unresolved issues with my mother, who is, my greatest pillar of support. Fun, stress, and anger are my triggers.

Non-lineal journey of recovery

I was a peer at Club HEAL since Day 1 in 2012 and became a volunteer, then a Publications Executive and then an Editor/Writer. Between 2012 to 2015, I had been free of hospitalisations, but I started having relapses from 2016 to 2018. I have since recovered from the last episode after which I resigned as I wanted to focus on healing at all levels.

Forgiveness is key

On the emotional level, I forgave all those who have hurt me in the past, especially my mother-in-law and my ex-husband. I forgave my mother for all the good and bad deeds, past or present, intentional, or not, real or imagined towards me. I forgave and love her unconditionally, knowing that as a mother, she loves me without conditions, and has done countless things for me from cooking to accompanying me to the psychiatrist. She stood by me, unashamed at my most embarrassing deeds. My relationship had taken a beating because of my numerous manic episodes when I had been reckless with my relationships with men and money. I saw her concern and over-protectiveness as controlling. I understand that caregivers have an extremely difficult time and it can be a rollercoaster ride for the whole family.

Its impact on my children has been equally devastating and I am still mending our relationships. This recent period of stability has been heaven-sent. I would say that healing from the hurt, anger, and grudges that I had with my mother was the main factor in my present well-being. She had been my trigger point, so much so that my psychiatrist and my supervisor at work recommended I stay at Simei Care Centre. When I realised that *I* decide who and what are my trigger points and take responsibility for managing them, then healing is possible. Finally, I forgave myself for all my wrongdoings and 'mistakes' and accept them as learning experiences which have made me the person I am today. Forgiveness is the key to Wellness.

Growing spiritually

Another factor that contributed to my recovery is my spiritual development where I renewed ties with my Creator. I connect every thought, emotion, and experience to God. I learn to live and let God. I believe in His Love and Wisdom and trust Him to guide me. I seek to do good to all His creations, be charitable, pray, meditate, contemplate, pursue knowledge, and draw closer to Him. I live in the present breath that He has gifted to me and do not dwell in the past nor the future. I value myself, my family and my friends and my fellowmen regardless of differences which are created by Him, only so that we can know each other. I believe in healing myself and healing the world.

ECTs and medications

Finally, in my recovery, I worked with my counsellor and a peer support specialist both of whom gave me valuable insights into my condition. They guided and walked with me through the healing process. I also followed my psychiatrists' advice in having daily oral medications, monthly injections, and outpatient Electroconvulsive Therapy (ECT). I steadfastly make my way to and back from IMH, a good two-hour journey from my home. I have a serious side-effect from one of my injections - severe tremors over my entire body. It is debilitating and embarrassing. But my doctor has reduced the dosage and we agreed to reduce it another time in December. I work with my doctor to manage my recovery and I listen to her just as she listens to my concerns.

A worthwhile contribution

I am thankful for my good health has allowed me to contribute again to Club HEAL since August last year, as a part-time Rehab Executive conducting Expressive Therapy and as a Freelance Writer. I have learnt to pace myself and being at peace has greatly enhanced my work. Healing from wounds of the past takes time and with healing only is recovery or absence of symptoms possible. Yet, I know recovery can go back and forth between its various stages, making relapse always a possibility. But I must remain positive and courageous.

To all those facing mental health challenges, be grateful that you have been chosen to be the heroes and heroines to inspire others including 'normal' folks who have their own challenges, be it mental, physical, emotional or spiritual. We are all in this together and let us encourage each other to be patient for we believe there is good in everything; yes, even the Covid-19.

AFTERWORD

I began this project expecting many tales of courage expressed through a mindset of patience and gratitude and I have not been disappointed. In fact, I am incredibly inspired by these stories of healing and recovery, most of which have taken time and are still ongoing.

All of them, through their different backgrounds and life experiences, have interesting tales to share on the healing process. One common theme they express is that the path towards wellness is not an easy one and takes considerable effort and time. In fact, none of the peers claim to have reached that elusive state of being recovered as they still experience their symptoms from time to time, and go in and out of different stages of recovery many times, not in a linear fashion. For example, having experienced a relapse, they can quickly bounce back into wellness, perhaps with counselling or therapy. Then they may have further relapses down the road.

Healing though is easier to experience than recovery as you regain the sense of self of who you were before the illness and are free to grow into a new and better, happier, and more contented human being. It is about being able to forgive those who hurt you and move on. It is about counting the blessings and appreciating the lessons learnt from the tragedies, traumas, and challenges in life.

Often, it is the journey itself that teaches them the meaning of patience and gratitude as they strive to make sense of their plight. Being imprisoned and suffering from addictions, having physically debilitating and incurable Illnesses, and experiencing abusive pasts – all this cause long drawn suffering that can only be relieved with a whole lot of patience and gratitude.

Some have expressed their pain and hopes through writing, such as penning their thoughts and feelings in their journals, and not a few do it through beautiful works of art like poetry, photography and paintings.

The individuals featured here have different beliefs that aid them in their recovery, but the majority are Muslims and find great relief and inspiration from Islam through the Qur'an and the traditions of Prophet Muhammad (peace be upon him). I personally feel the impact of these words as I struggle to make sense of my own trials and tribulations. I reiterate and end with one of these quotes that has seen me through 22 years of mental health challenges:

The Prophet Muhammad (pbuh) said:

How amazing is the affair of the believer! Everything is good for him – and that is for no one but the believer: If good times come his way, he is thankful and that is good for him, and if hardship comes his way he is patient and that is good for him.
[*Muslim*]

ABOUT THE AUTHOR

Yohanna Abdullah is a well-established writer in Singapore focusing on mental health issues. The former Journalist with The Straits Times has dedicated her time and passion with Club HEAL, a charity aimed at improving the quality of life for people with mental health challenges. She struggles with bipolar disorder since 1998 which has given her a unique view of life. Leveraging on her education in Sociology, English Language and Philosophy and rich work experiences in media and communications, she is a mental health advocate, scriptwriter, playwright, editor, novelist, and poet. The nature-lover is a single mother of two children and a happy grandaunt.

ABOUT CLUB HEAL

Club HEAL is a charity in Singapore established in 2012 that promotes the healing and recovery of people with mental health challenges by inspiring Hope, Empowering lives, fostering Acceptance and spreading Love. It has a vision of a stigma-free society that is conducive for healing and recovery. Services provided by Club HEAL include day rehabilitative services, counselling, home visits, public education, support groups and volunteer training.